Kindergarten Education

This is an astonishing, impressive and magnificent work. Astonishing in the expansive vision it offers and scope of its material synthesized and offered with such clarity. It is also heartbreaking in that the world of childhood offered is so perfectly in tune with 'Nature's Imperative' for child development while so dramatically different from what is happening to the vast majority of children world-wide. Peck's offering could very literally save us from the suicidal path currently pursued by our 'collective cultural imperative.' The phrase 'this is must reading' has been overused, but surely this is must reading for every parent, would-be parent, and teacher world-wide. I would couple it with Tobin Hart's magnificent gem 'The Secret Spiritual World of Childhood,' just published by Inner Oceans. Peck provides the grounds for a true spiritual awakening in each child, and so in our species as a whole. I can only praise the work and pray it will be widely read.

Joseph Chilton Pearce, author of *Magical Child*
Evolution's End
The Biology of Transcendence

Kindergarten Education

Freeing children's creative potential

Betty Peck

Hawthorn Press

Published by Hawthorn Press, Hawthorn House, 1 Lansdown Lane, Stroud, Gloucestershire, GL5 1BJ, UK
Tel: (01453) 757040 Fax: (01453) 751138
info@hawthornpress.com
www.hawthornpress.com

Cover photograph by Charlie Bryan and Lucy Craven
Illustrations by Marije Rowling
Cover design by Hawthorn Press
Typesetting by Hawthorn Press, Stroud, Glos.
Printed in the UK by The Cromwell Press, Trowbridge, Wiltshire

Printed on acid-free paper from managed forests

Every effort has been made to trace the ownership of all copyrighted material. If any omission has been made, please bring this to the publisher's attention so that proper acknowledgment may be given in future editions.

Saratoga community garden painting by Helen Caswell
Stained glass window by Sarah and Joel Hirschfeld's mother
Old Befana drawing by Anne Eisley
School House painting by Dale Barron and his mother

British Library Cataloguing in Publication Data applied for

ISBN 1 903458 33 1

Contents

I dedicate this book to my daughter, Anna Rainville,
and my son, Bill Peck, whose dramatic talent
has enriched us all, and my wonderful husband,
Willys Peck, who makes it all possible.

Acknowledgements

Besides the parents and students of my years of teaching, my inspiration has come from many sources over the years. Dorothea Chappell, a devotee of Maria Montessori, opened up the world of music for me as a young parent. Alan Chadwick opened up the world of gardening to me. In my conversations with Buckminster Fuller, the world's structure and oneness became mine. Emilia Rathun opened up the depth of spirituality that I claim as my own. I wish every teacher of the young child could have experienced Margret Meyerkort's classroom and experienced her dedication to the essence of education. I am truly grateful for her inspiration.

Elizabeth Murray has shown the way beauty of the garden vibrates with the oneness of the universe in our daily lives. Everyone needs the inspiration of a Justine Forbes to believe in them.

Nancy Mellon has inspired in me the cultivation of the art of storytelling.

Experiencing my daughter Anna Rainville sail through life bringing an artistic depth to all of us whose life she touches is the essence of inspiration for me. I cannot forget Friedrich Froebel, Rudolf Steiner, and Maria Montessori, who have confirmed my intuitive understanding of my work with the young child.

I wish to thank Marv Steinberg for the invitation to create a Kindergarten at the Saratoga School. I want to thank my computer gurus Don Armstrong, Roy Crawford, and Bill Kalageros for their help. I am truly thankful for Kathryn Mathewson's, Rebecca Dye's, Hank Helbush's, and Nancy Payne's love of gardening that has enriched the lives of us all. Thank yous to the Mert Parons of this world whose love of life flows through their gift of giving. I want to thank Betty Kuhar for the gift of beauty to my life and Kitty Maguire and Pat Fox for their artistic touch. My thanks for many musical celebrations to Lee Ann Welch, fiddler. My thanks also to Walter Kool for his help with pictures. A special thank you for Esperanza Garcia's help and an extra special thank you to my helper Jade Bradbury, as well as to all those who have made this book possible.

Foreword

by Cathy Nutbrown

This book is something of a treasure. To read it is to open up an old trunk and find it filled with mementoes which trigger memories of voices, touches, smells, events and people. It is intensely personal in its account of the practices and philosophy of one woman, yet it is brimming too with opportunities for any teacher of young children to connect with experiences of their own.

This story, a patchwork of many, many stories of Kindergarten life with young children and their families, brought to mind the opening words of Robert Fulghum's famous essay. He wrote:

'All I really need to know
about how to live and what to do
and how to be
I learned in kindergarten.' [1]

The essay goes on to demonstrate how the basic lessons of life are laid out in the early years, and how ways of being in later life are underpinned by the experiences and lessons in the beginning years. This book provides further account of that belief.

What a joy to find a book filled with celebrations! But not 'just' celebrations – blessing too, and in abundance. In particular, the final blessing: *'Blessings on all teachers who know that to nourish their own spirit is the greatest gift of the child.'*

Given the pace of development and change in early childhood education and care in many parts of the world, it is important for those who work with young children to remember that they must 'nourish themselves' in order to do the best job they can in their work with children. And part of that nourishment is, to use Robert Fulghum's words, to 'be aware of wonder'. Kindergarten teachers will not all choose Betty Peck's ways of sharing and celebrating her wonders of life, but what they will surely take from her story is the importance of finding ways to look, and listen and learn and celebrate life and all its surprises. The British summer of 2003 in the UK was long and hot and dry, and the sun left a gift of rich, rich reds and golds in the Autumn leaves, something to wonder at and celebrate. Betty Peck says that education is all about leaves, and there are many different leaves, many shapes, textures and colours – and so it is with teaching kindergarten. Each teacher is unique and does things in his or her own different way; but what distinguishes a special teacher is their constant belief in the spirit of childhoods.

I should like to think that this unique book is not necessarily *that* unique. For I should like to think that there are many who have worked with young children for a lifetime who too could also write *their* story, and whose pupils could testify to the life-forming nature of the experience they had in kindergarten. What is clear in these pages is that in giving so fully and richly of one's self, blessings flow and enrich the giver. Betty Peck has given us a book which deserves to be on the kitchen table, thumbed and read, a little now, a little then. There are moments to marvel at, moments to shed tears over, moments to argue with and moments to be amazed at. It is a call to celebrate life with young children and to help them to find their own ways to open their souls to beauty.

As the rhythm of the seasons reminds us again that the world is turning, this book is a kind of Springtime; refreshing and full of vitality, coming as it does from a lifetime of work and commitment. And with the Spring comes an opportunity for another blessing:

'As we celebrate Spring's returning and the rejuvenation of the natural world.

'Let us be moved by this vast and gentle insistence that goodness shall return, that warmth and life shall succeed, and help us to understand our place within this miracle.

'Let us see that as a bird now builds its nest, bravely, with bits and pieces, so we must build human faith. It is our simple duty; it is the highest art; it is our natural and vital role within the miracle of spring; the creation of faith '[2]

I have never met Betty Peck, but her book has given me the opportunity to get to know her. To ask questions, to agree passionately, and to argue too! Keep your copy on the kitchen table and enjoy its riches from time to time.

Dr. Cathy Nutbrown
University of Sheffield, UK
November 2003

1 Fulghum, R. (1990) *All I really need to know I learned in Kindergarten* New York: Villard Books

2 Michel Lueing (1997) *Book of prayers* New York: Milling Press

Introduction

What can children gather in the treasured world of childhood that will enrich and bring meaning to their adult lives? The Greek word for childhood was one and the same with the word *play.* It is in play that you develop your initiative. All your wonderful ideas prove to be different ways of using methods of problem-solving. Your ability to transform things is polished. You are in charge of the world and yourself as you 'try on' the culture. In one sense you are what you are today as a result of moments of free play that were yours when you were young.

The teacher knows that the less perfect the material used in play, the more the child will bring to complete it with his or her imagination. That is why sand, water, and rocks are the best of all play materials. Everything the child touches must resonate with integrity.

Because humans are designed to live in a garden, it is here that children find a world that feeds their senses. The colours, the smells, the tastes, the feeling of new life, and the sense of death that they experience here will be theirs forever. In the garden the child experiences the great law of nature, which says that all things are all things. He feels no separation. He, then, can take upon himself the guardianship of all he touches. With this step comes a feeling of *gratitude,* upon which all social feeling is cultivated: One builds upon the other. Without the feeling of gratitude, the child cannot know what it means to be truly human. It is no wonder that Friedrich Froebel gave the word 'Kindergarten' to the world of the five-year-old child.

When Froebel set up his classes for the four-, five-, and six-year-old child, he did not want to call it the Infant School, as other classes of young children were called in his day – for it was not a 'school' that was needed by the child. This age did not belong in a school setting, but rather in a garden. Here, Froebel thought, was the natural setting for the child to gather all he needed. His classes were called Kindergartens, German for child *(kinder)* and garden *(garten).*

In the Kindergarten the rhythm of the seasons carries the child. She moves to the rhythm of the beat in each experience: in poetry, in song, in the names of her friends, and in the chants that come when she is with her friends, holding hands and moving in a circle of singing games.

In other words, the child develops at the age of five in the way that early man himself developed. It's a time of discovery, a time of believing fairy tales that are truer than true. It's a time when the unity of the human being and the natural world is seen and experienced. It is here in the fairy tale where you are free to meet joy, sorrow, and all manner of feelings of wonder and reverence. Here seeds of true gratitude, responsibility, and loving care are planted.

So many children have been torn out of the imaginative world and plunged into the mundane of the everyday without being given whole new tapestries within which they can find their own path. Rich is the person who has known a spinner of tales, whose imagination nourishes the listener at every level. Perhaps the ability to make pictures in the mind and to know that things need never stay the same is one of the most important gifts that childhood can bring to their adult life.

The ability to record experiences and to create the world all over again belongs to the five-year-old. The only word we have for this process is art. For the child of five there is never enough paint, crayons, paste, and paper. The aim of education is to produce artists. The child must feel the sense of the beautiful brought into the heart of all that is learned.

Nothing should be torn from its wholeness and connectedness to all other things. The child must hold arithmetic in her hands and feel the wholeness from which come the numbers that have meaning in her life.

All of early man's words were pictures. Often the child feels as early humans felt when the Phoenicians had reduced their pictures to lines: It was as though they were looking at something demonic. We are here as teachers to put back the life forces into all of learning, but especially the letters human beings use for their language. Celebration accompanies the occasion of learning to write and to know a letter that can mysteriously hold not only a sound, but a heartbeat.

As writing appropriately precedes reading, so movement to the sound precedes writing. When the child has learned to read everything, he will be ready with both 'roots and wings' for the years ahead, when the world is reduced to reading pages of black-and-white print. He will then be rich in imagination, beauty, rhythm, gratitude, and the ways of discovery and wonder, which have been founded in play, singing games, fairy tales, and in a garden that has been his.

One should endeavour to meet the child with the right timing on every level of growth during these early years. The understanding of why we do certain things is important for the adult. The 'why' is the reason the parent must be involved, along with the Kindergarten child, in this, the Kindergarten year.

I say, as Carl Jung said when he was asked if he believed in God, 'I do not believe; I *know*'. And so I know that the parent is the true educator for the child. The parent must therefore have the oldest of the old and the newest of the new insight into all that nourishes both himself as a parent and his Kindergarten child. This book tells of my experience in celebrating all of life with four-, five-, and six-year-old children and their parents. Lucky is the family which enters the Kindergarten and feels the teacher to be life-giving. How important it is to feel the reverence, joy, gratitude, and responsibility that fills every word and gesture of the teacher.

I believe that the concept of 'All things are all things' can be presented with beauty on all levels – helping the child in her celebration of life. Knowing this interrelatedness of herself and the earth, herself and the cosmos, herself and all learning, really does provide the child with both roots and wings.

Put differently, we can say that the teacher is like the Great Mother – the Great Cosmic Force. And because the child does not want to be separated from this order, he moves into place, because now is the time to do certain things separately from parents' or teachers' whim or desire. At no other time in his life will this be the pattern between student and teacher. Oral literature is now attached to all rhythm and movement – chanting, clapping, walking, and stamping. Poetry glows with aliveness to the beat. Nothing is taken in that does not have its celebration – getting into it and becoming part of it.

All stories connect these children to the earth – where the creatures talk with us and the plants call us by name. We use stories that include repeated phrases and groupings of objects over and over again – such repetitions creating a calming, stabilizing rhythm. For example, first he said goodnight to the cat, then the dog, and so on; then the farmer drank some warm milk and went to bed. This rhythm nourishes the child on all levels of development.

The year is filled with fairy tales – full of feeling sad, full of feeling joy, fear, laughter, hope, and anticipation. All the stories are told with joyous imagination, enriching the child with great truths with which to live for ever.

The teacher knows that the forming of pictures in the mind of the child precedes all of the other work presented. It was from this foundation that early man began, for as we know, the first writings were pictures. But even before this, each new experience and object he discovered found within him a corresponding movement. Life forces came to the sounds that form our language. And out of this comes the form of the letters which we celebrate with feasts and pageantry in the Kindergarten. We will be building the foundation to move from picture to symbols which will help us to fly through the thoughts of man on the printed page. This makes us able to use these words as our own as we reach out to others.

The teacher knows that it is in numbers that we feel the rhythm of the universe and we can therefore trustingly rest, knowing the security of its great mathematical genius. Our Kindergarten arithmetic is based on our bodies, the garden, and all that relates to the wholeness of the moment. It is then that we can divide, give away, add, and multiply in imaginative ways that contain the fundamental truths of these disciplines.

Every year it is my goal that the teacher and the parents work together to see that the deep integrity of all materials, stories, songs, poetry, and everything that fills our days is worthy of the child at this stage of his lawful development – his imitative stage.

When children walk through the garden gate into my Kindergarten room, where they will be from September until the following June, I want them not only to feel connected with truth, which wears the crown of beauty, but that their growing in the Kindergarten will resonate with some distant womb whose timing was also nine months.

A few words are in order about my own professional history and development. As I now feel the need to help other Kindergarten teachers meet the challenges that are brought to the teaching field today, my daughter, Anna Rainville, and I have established the Kindergarten Forum. The Forum is held every Solstice and Equinox during the year. Speakers are brought in to focus on the topic of the day, and there is always a craft presented to the teachers to enrich the day's topic.

After I retired from teaching, I worked on my Doctor of Education degree, choosing a programme that demanded that the candidate be active in the field of their choice. I worked with the County Office of Education in setting up a programme for the enrichment of Kindergarten teachers. My practicum was titled, 'Cultivating Beauty in an Integrated Aesthetic Program that Meets the Needs of the Child'. The Doctorate programme took three years. After meeting together every Monday for that length of time in the program I designed, the teachers wanted to continue in some way – and it was then that the Kindergarten Forum was established.

During my years of Kindergarten teaching, I felt that the children of our area needed the exposure to the earth in a meaningful way that would enliven their lives on every level. Alan Chadwick, at the University of California at Santa Cruz, had developed a remarkable bio-dynamic, French-intensive, organic garden. In the early 1970s, he agreed to come over and start a garden at our school. We set up a lecture for the teachers and administration, and because Alan Chadwick was trained as a Shakespearean actor, he had no trouble at all in greatly impressing the entire staff. At that time no one knew anything about the organic way… in fact some of the teachers were a little afraid of this method. Since the trustees of the school were afraid of vandalism, they took it to the City Council to sponsor. Mayor Jerry Smith said, 'Yes, go out, Betty, and find the land. If we don't own it, we'll rent it.' And so we walked all over our town trying to find the right spot for such a garden. My friend Ruth Langwill took Alan and me to a piece of property near her house. The property was owned by the Odd Fellows Lodge. This small valley had once been a farm, and it was here where a beautiful 10-acre garden was established. I took my Kindergarten children out to this garden every Monday. We were all part of this new organic method that had been brought to our city of Saratoga, and is now spreading nation-wide.

The school that I had started several years earlier for my own children on the Easterbrook Farm is still going after all these years; in a different location. This training school for parents still invites me back to give lectures and be a part of their celebrations.

This school, now called the Los Gatos Saratoga Observation Nursery School, was inspired by my training in the British Infant School in 1950. Soon after my work in Britain, I was hired by the San Mateo County Department of Education to be a supervisor for Kindergarten, and first through third grades. I set up a programme in the Kindergarten where teachers could watch for three days as I taught the class. I soon discovered that it would take more than three days, so I opened my own Kindergarten Demonstration School, sponsored by the local American Association of University Women. Before this, I had three years training in teaching parents at a preschool in Palo Alto under Bess Bolton. Finally, last but not least, I was blessed by being born the oldest of six children, which was the perfect training for a Kindergarten teacher.

PART I

The Ethos Pervading the Living Kindergarten

The Rhythm of the Day and the Week

The rhythmic pulse of life is needed on every level, but never so much as in Kindergarten, as every teacher and child knows. It is in the rhythm of the universe that we find our connections to life, which is the birthright of every child. The rhythm of the day and week that has evolved with my years of teaching reached perfection in dividing the class. The early group came at 8:30 and went home at 12; the other children came at 10 and stayed for lunch and went home at 2.

Every morning we start with the cocktail hour where children come in and visit with each other before they are called to the **MOON BOAT**. (I call it the moon boat because the seating is in the shape of a crescent moon.) When we are seated in our chairs, the count is taken and written down. We first tally the count at the first of the year, then change it to finger numbers, and after the first of the year we use Indo-Arabic numbers and take a beautifully presented account of how many children are present down to the office.

It is here in the MOON BOAT that we have the songs and poetry that set the mood for the telling of the fairy tale of the week. The fairy tale becomes a play on Friday. A song leads us over to the indoor garden. It is here where we chart the moon and take on the glow of the season; it is here where we count the days to birthdays, full moon, holidays, and so on, where we chant our poetry of the season, where we look at the gifts that now belong to the garden, and are grateful as we acknowledge Mother Earth or old King Winter, who sit in their costume ready to have us taste of the gifts of the season. We move with song to the centre that houses our sound of the week. The sound is presented with story and drawings that open up movement and rhythmical activities. We document in every way possible: it is here we relate the Indo-Arabic numbers to our bodies to be used in all activities after the first of the year.

The morning class then greets the afternoon children at 10. If it is Monday, we go on a field trip to the Community Garden to gather everything that starts with our sound for the week, bury ourselves in the seasonal activities of the garden and watch people who love the earth working in all areas of the garden.

On Tuesday, Wednesday, and Thursday, mother helpers come. We divide into groups of six. It is within the groups that the world of numbers and sounds expands into artistic, meaningful activities. We make books with magic doors that house the picture of the story of the week, and pictures of words that start with the sound are drawn. Here we take the symbol of the week and find it in all we see and make. Thus, with the spiral – when we stir the cake batter, look at a snail, cut around the '0' making a rounded path to its centre. Then we draw it, make it with clay, find it in the rose, the calla lily, and hear the story of how it lives in our bodies. It is in the small group that the letter of the week is recognized in our bodies, garden or outside world. The cookie-dough mother has sent in dough to form a letter-shaped cookie each week, and it is baked and eaten so that it becomes a part of us in a very real way.

After these jobs are done we work on our tasks that must also be taken in order of our development – sequencing, matching more or less space relationships, and so on. One of the groups cooks each day.

Arithmetical concepts of dividing, adding, multiplying, and taking-away are presented in story form and acted out each day… from the whole to its parts, as Rudolf Steiner advocated. Number building is presented, relating to important events in our lives. Numbers to 100 are written when needed for celebrations, comparing and contrasting them with our own special numbers that relate to our family.

Creative play time comes at 11 o'clock, indoors or out in the garden. Play is the most important part of the day. It is in creative play that the child experiences her world by trying on the culture. Then there are singing games when we gather together in the Golden Ring.

Every seasonal game is about the sound of the week or death, birth, marriage, number, birthday celebration, or nature songs that we sing and move to in rhythmic fashion.

On Thursday, we all come early and go home at 12, and we make bread. This is also our garden day, when we care for our garden. A King or Queen of ecology is chosen, and when we gather for a ceremony we eat a warm loaf of our bread, thanking the earth for its kindness to us.

On Mondays, we paint with water colours. We use only three colours to find the rainbow of colours on wet paper with song and ceremony. Water colours come with the rain in January when all things are new; up to this time we have used poster paint.

We have wool from our sheep that we clean, spin, and dye in the autumn and then use all year long. We have cotton from the cotton plant we have in our room. And we raise silkworms so that we can thank them for our silk that we use for our plays, etc. Everything in our room must come from the source: raw material.

On Fridays, we celebrate the sound of the week. We eat things that start with the sound at our sound parties, on doilies that we make showing the picture of the sound and something that starts with the sound on the other side. Each week we have special music to go with the singing games. We sit around in our Golden Ring with our special plates chosen on our first day of school. With these plates we learn the orderly fashion of numbers that mark where we sit in the Golden Ring.

Then there is the closing ceremony. Every child gets his special hug goodbye, lifting-off-their-feet hug, an arms-around-the-neck hug, a hug that needs no words as to the importance in the life of the child and the adult. My father always lifted me off my feet with his hug. The afternoon children who stay for lunch wash their hands in the Silver Sea... singing, Dry, Hands, Dry... and run to picnic under the trees with Jenni Tayler, my aide.

There can only be an artistic Kindergarten programme filled with beauty if the teacher knows *the reason behind* the Golden Ring, the music and singing games, the Moon Boat, the numbers, the sounds, the garden, the shapes, the fairy tales, work, death, birth, birthdays, bread, cooking, the need to celebrate the seasons, the dress of the teacher, the chosen mother-teachers of the room, the creative play, the furniture, the form of the room, the development of the child, the crafts, the writing, the rhythm, the colour, the toys, the healing basket, and the intuitive nature of the healthy child that seeks its resonance in the intuitive nature of the teacher; and this takes a lifetime of study and experience.

Real Work

It is so important to give the children a taste of helping to carry on the work of the world. The teacher's ability to find 'real work' is a vital need in the Kindergarten. How important it is that the Kindergarten children link themselves with the finest examples of manhood and womanhood. This is the Kindergarten child's real work – to imitate what is seen by the child. This identification with 'greatness' is the concern of the Kindergarten teacher.

One of the forms of real work is producing a play each week. The dress-ups, the stage setting, and the choosing of characters demand the whole attention of the class, together with the creative outlay of projecting into our lives the reality of the story. We must at that moment transform everything that we have into the vital flow of the fairy tale. The blue silks become the river; the wooden blocks form the gate to the castle. You see the children wrapping themselves in browns and greens, standing on chairs to be the tallest trees in the forest. This is their real world, and it is up to the teacher to see that it is enjoyed and provided for each week. It is also necessary to step into the role of worker on their level. One has to look around and see what is needed to be done in the surrounding area of the Kindergarten.

Some children come from situations that could use help with their family's activities. Jeremy and Jenni come from the Congress Springs Winery. During the harvest season we are invited up to harvest the grapes. We work alongside the grape pickers and put our grapes in their buckets, and we hear their beautiful language – Spanish – filling the air. We have learned all year some Spanish from Susan, our Spanish mother, so that we are able greet them and tell them our names.

We say our thank-yous for letting us help them. We are filling ourselves on every level. We eat the grapes and feel the warm sun in the juice itself, and our eyes take in the colours of harvest. We feel the rain in the juice of the grapes, and we see the redness of the colour as it stains our hands, clothes, and mouths. We see the grapes leave the vine and travel in buckets and large carrying containers that leave the vineyard. Then they are pressed into large vats. We are invited to stir the grapes, where the sun now holds hands with the rain, wind, and minerals. It is here that all the seasons, with moonshine and star shine, have given birth to this moment. And now it is the touch of human hands that is needed to work together to produce this juice of the vine, and we, the Kindergarten, are a part of this process. In the early winter we are invited back to the vineyard to see the pruning of the vines. We take these prunings and turn them into wreaths – they become our gifts.

Then in spring we are invited by Jenni's and Jeremy's family to come and play in the mustard in early spring. When they greet us, it is with pure joy that we are welcomed. Jenni and Jeremy's parents are warm, loving people, who can't think of anything more wonderful than the Kindergarten arriving with our buckets to harvest the grapes, make our wreaths, and roll in the mustard. They welcome us with open arms, thus setting the tone for our adventure into the world of seasons and the relatedness of the love that is involved in working with the earth, along with hard work.

A vital need for real work occurred when a delivery of white rock arrived at our local Japanese garden which is a city park. To his horror, the gardener saw that, mixed with the white rock was black rock. The Kindergarten children immediately came to the rescue, and many a field trip was organized to help pick out the black rock. This is a Kindergarten task of sorting out; that is a real need of the developing child. Here was our real work designed for us, and we felt more than needed. We used these black rocks in many ways in our Kindergarten maths.

In the autumn we listen for walnut trees in the area to call our names. Who needs help to harvest their walnuts? We have never been without walnuts in our cooking, gift-giving, or treats in our Kindergarten. The owners are always pleased to have their walnuts harvested, and we therefore bring our buckets home full of walnuts.

But we bring back more than the walnuts. We bring back the memories of the smiles on Matthew's mother's face. I first saw that beautiful smile on that mother's face when she brought her two boys to the Kindergarten. And now they are grown, and they carry on the work of the farm. These two farmers were often there to greet us as our class arrived to help them with their work.

We visited this farm again when the cherries were in blossom, and for our cherry picking in June. We picked and ate as many as we could, standing on the ground. They always left a few for us to harvest. After we filled ourselves with cherries, we gave the rest for our hostess to sell. When we came for another visit, Brian had made a cake that said 'Thank you for the year'. For it is important to visit in autumn, winter, spring, and the days closest to summer when you visit a farm.

We all gathered around on Natalie's handmade quilt and ate cake and the rest of our cherries, stuffing ourselves with spring itself. These were our cherries and our cherry trees. We claimed them as our own.

In the Saratoga Community Garden we always had real work, according to the season when the Kindergarten class would have their field trip. Picking up the black walnuts, opening up the bean pods, sending the flowers back to Mother Earth, picking raspberries, harvesting wheat. Lucky indeed is the child who knows the real work of a garden. It is never ending. Like everything else, you have to find a stopping-place. There is never enough real work in the Kindergarten. How does a teacher bring to the life of the child the feeling of 'feeling needed'? How does the child enter into 'Man's Estate', as my husband calls it?

We want the Kindergarten child to feel the joy of real work, which is his birthright, and to feel this joy for ever! I have known men who found the joy and dignity that hard work can bring. Mr. Hardy was a prince of a man. He felt it an honour to clean the Kindergarten room. What could he fix today? It was as though the king himself had found his life's work in making the Kindergarten a better, cleaner, and safer place to be. He had beautiful posture that gave grace to all the needs of cleaning. He was every Kindergarten teacher's dream. He spoke with authority in a quiet way, and you knew that no matter how the Kindergarten had piled itself to the ceiling that day, he would restore it to beauty.

Our ten-acre Saratoga Community Garden, where we spent the day each Monday, was filled with meaningful work for the Kindergarten child. This garden was a biodynamic, French-intensive, demonstration garden started when I asked Alan Chadwick to come over and help us start a garden. Every teacher realizes the value of uniting Kindergarten children in the same experience on Monday. They come from many different environments and need to feel the foundation that will be used for that week in Kindergarten.

One Monday, we arrived back at school from the visit to this garden to find the leaves from our catalpa tree being taken away in black carry-all bags by the gardeners. I stood there with the children, at first shocked that anyone was so ill-informed that they would rob of us of our leaves, which were the basis of our life-giving curriculum. I stood there and shouted, 'Give us back our leaves', in the most powerful voice I could muster. Then the children began, 'Give us back our leaves!'. The men were bewildered, and they emptied the sacks of our leaves, and we cheered.

What do you think education is? Certainly not sitting with paper and pencil. It's *leaves!*

WE LOVE LEAVES!

We play in the leaves.
We walk in the leaves.
We sing about leaves.
We say poems about leaves.
We sleep in the leaves, hoping to be kissed by a leaf.
We cover ourselves with leaves.

We tell stories about leaves.
We dance and fall like the leaves.
We trace them.
We draw them.
We press them.
We design with them.
We rake them into piles.
We have conversations about leaves.
We count the leaves.
We weigh the leaves.
We play games with the leaves.
We compare and contrast the leaves.
We line them up in order of size.
We were waiting for the first rains to carry them down to us.
We have waited and counted the days for them to fall.
We've watched them turn the magic colour of our floor.
We love the sound our five-year-old feet make as we move in them.
We explore them to see how quiet they are when the rain comes.
We learn the letter 'L' first, which is found in the lifeline of every leaf.
WE LOVE LEAVES.
We gather them up in our arms.
We take them home in our pockets.

Having a catalpa tree and sycamore trees is a child's paradise. It's what childhood is all about. To be in leaves, to feel them, to know you can count on them to know how to change and fall, to feel needed in their effort to return to the earth, is pure joy. How important we feel to rescue them from the blacktop and tuck them in the beautiful compost bin. It is here in the compost that all the promiscuous insects and creatures too hard to see work all winter, turning them into new earth. Then we watch this new earth alive with life become a part of our vegetable beds, where we will grow our seeds. It is here we will gather our vegetables to eat on celebration days, having discovered that all things are all things.

Our leaves are our life. These leaves have been giving us our oxygen during the three hours we have been at school each day. We have been exchanging our breath with them. They have needed us and we have needed them. We are now putting them to rest in our garden. We carry them with great effort in the wheelbarrow, parading after one another with our rakes, brooms, and shovels. This is the way we show our gratitude for the days we spent in their shade and the days we watched them with joy dancing in the wind. This is how we show our gratitude for the days spent feeling their life and beauty through our schoolroom window.

And now we will be waiting for the last leaf to fall. This is a moment of awe, which is always carefully recorded. And then there is the long wait to see if the tree will live again. Has it died, or will there be new leaves again? When you're five years old, new life of spring is a celebration. Then we watch them grow until they welcome summer with their cascades of white blossoms. At this very moment, all summer-born children celebrate their birthdays.

The celebration of the seasons is man's birthright. This is what we are all about, and each year I have to scream to protect the rights of the five-year-old to real education.

Gratitude

The gratefulness of the teacher for all of life must be felt by the child. How lucky is the child to have a teacher whose feeling of gratefulness spills over to the Kindergarten. Grateful that these children were chosen for her. Thankful for all the problems that come her way, for she knows this is where vital learning takes place. Thankful for each day that finds her actively involved in the interchange of the child, parents, administration, materials, school buildings, and colleagues, and with the beauty of poems, stories, songs, dances, drama, and art. Gratitude is the foundation of all learning. I want the children to feel this gratefulness of soul, for it is the children who renew this attitude each day for the teacher.

The young child spills over with gratefulness. One only has to look into his eyes to see this gratefulness that as yet knows no words. However, to keep alive this magic of reverence and thankfulness, one needs to build up a reservoir of images through stories, poems, songs, singing games, experiences, dramas, and plays that deal with being thankful. Providing opportunities for this was what the month of November was all about in our Kindergarten.

We start our celebration of gratitude by knowing that here, in Saratoga, we are blessed with an Indian name. The name of our town starts our relationship to the past when the North American Indians walked here in our Kindergarten garden long ago. The introduction begins with the story of Tribe-Boy. This story tells an imaginative adventure of how the drum was discovered. It gives to the children the appreciation of everyone who was involved in this great event, as well as allowing them to connect themselves to something greater than themselves.

There is a feeling of awe that comes over the children when the great drum we have in our room is uncovered each year. This is one of the beginning November steps of gratefulness. Our drum was made by one of our local Native Americans, Big Buffalo. When I invited him to make a drum for us, he told me then that I had to wait until he found the right skin to make the drum. It was in Spring that he entered our school with a touch of traditional garb carrying the drum. He had chosen a deep Indian red for the exterior of the drum, which was 30 inches in diameter.

Our new principal, the prince who now wears the crown, sent a messenger out to the garden to tell me that the drum had arrived. He wanted me to bring the children in to have our pictures taken with Big Buffalo. 'No', I said. 'But I will come to hear Big Buffalo call Spring.' I brought my children in from the garden and we gathered around him as he called Spring's name. 'Spring... Spring... Spring....' The drum called out Spring's name over and over again as the children chanted to the drum beat. Then I asked him to call our Indian name of Sar-a-to-ga. Our voices joined together with the voice of the drum and the sound filled the school.

Then the maker of the drum began his own Indian tribal songs, with the drum responding with its thunderous rhythmic pulse that carried us into the heart of his native days of long ago. When he was finished, each child thanked the Indian drum maker one by one. They shook his hand and looked into the beautiful black Indian eyes that make all the history of our Saratoga Village come alive.

With this introduction, the drum was placed in our room. With each new class each year in the autumn, we look at the drum, remembering that it was made from one of Mother Earth's creatures. We say our 'thank-yous'. I then play the rhythm of each child's name on the drum. Hearing our names called out on the drum was the beginning of all our steps into design, number work, and dance. Thus our thankfulness began.

All the animals and folks who had made the drum had to be thanked in special drum music. Children took turns saying their thank-yous on the drum. We took the pattern, or beat of our name, and found our own name design. Cathryn's name became loud-soft, loud-soft, loud-soft. The other children chant and clap the rhythm of her name with her. This experience of hearing one's name being played on the drum brings a deep relatedness with all that has gone on before to make this moment possible. And it is this relatedness that brings the overwhelming joy of gratefulness.

Then Cathryn rises and dances to the music of her name. How will her feet find Cath-ryn's name? Because it is her own, the pattern easily absorbs her. Cathryn settles on a giant step and a short step. She dances around the room with everyone clapping to her Cathryn music. Now she can take paper and crayon and write her name exactly as she has heard it on the drum. She chooses a long line and a short line…. Then this changes to blue green… blue green… blue green. She has now gone from the real experience to the abstract. She finds herself able to hear the music of other names (syllables) and read everyone's design.

Images have now been built up in the children's minds through the story of Tribe-Boy and the story of the arrival of Big Buffalo, our Indian Drum Maker, who called Spring and sang his own song of thankfulness. With this we usher in the autumn season of the year. The entire season has spilled over into the room. The harvest is everywhere: apples, pomegranates, nuts, leaves, persimmons, cones – all the treasure houses of Mother Earth have been gathered for the beauty of this moment. The smells of autumn and the autumnal colours surround this important step in the child's life-pattern. The entrance into reading is first the reading of all life through smell, sounds, and tastes of autumn that will make words come alive when we are ready to make them our own.

We now move to an even more abstract form than we build on from the rhythmic pattern of the drum. Because the teacher knows the beginning steps that unlock arithmetic and reading, she knows it is important for the children to have played first with the material. She wants to establish the drum rhythm, using coloured blocks of all sizes and shapes spread out before the children. Everything must start with play. In this way they are bound to come across the ordered form of repeat design. Lucky is the child who has discovered this himself without the teacher showing him how to do it. We as teachers need to learn not to get in the way of the child's own discovery.

Then comes the day when a child does discover repeat design. I ask if I may read what Jenny has built: red-green, red-green, red-green, red-green…. She, too, is delighted in this calming rhythmic pattern that she chants to herself and others. Is there another way she would read it? It is only a matter of minutes until the two beats of the drum rhythm turn into her own name – Jen-ny, Jen-ny. When children see and hear this pattern of their own names, they return again and again to it with grateful joy. Then they begin to build other children's names:

Brian: red-orange, red-orange, red-orange.

An-dre-as: blue-white-green, blue-white-green, blue-white-green.

The child's unlocking of the joy of reading designs provides boundless freedom in all artistic areas. Necklaces can now be made telling a story. With a great supply of picked-up pods and cones (we call them Mother Earth treasure houses) and wooden beads, the child is free to tell his story or her history.

Each child has a different story to tell. Eric reads his Indian necklace. Four eucalyptus pods and a bead reads:

'My tooth is loose.' stopping dot.

'My tooth is loose.' stopping dot.

'My tooth is loose.' stopping dot.

Then Heather reads her Indian necklace:

'I love you.' stopping dot.

'I love you.' stopping dot.

'I love you.' stopping dot.

Melinda writes how old she is: 1 – 2 – 3 – 4 – 5, stopping dot. Six eucalyptus pods and then a bead.

Thus, as you see, the stopping dot/wooden bead becomes the period in the sentence structure of life's stories. How wonderful it is to feel the period in your hand as the wooden bead in your necklace. Children at this age can benefit from all the ideas a teacher can use to get life into grammar structure before they are faced with pencil and paper and the years of collecting all that has gone into making our language. Everything begins to take on the motif of repeat design.

Children find repeat designs everywhere – on buildings, boards, books, and so on. They bring repeat designs from home. We are reading these rhythmic patterns everywhere.

I like the children to be grateful for everything. I also want them to feel the connectedness they have to the earth.

THANK YOU

Mia Michael

Thank you, thank you, thank you ve- ry much.

Thank you, thank you, thank you ve- ry much.

On some lovely day in the autumn of the year when November rolls around, the beautiful oak chairs from the Kindergarten room are put out under the oak tree to form the Moon Boat. (I pity the Kindergarten teacher who has no elf helpers.) 'Where is the Moon Boat?', the children cry as they come into the room. 'You will have to find it', I say. They dash off trying to find it. When the children discover where the moon boat is, they are quite puzzled. Out under the great oak tree in the front of our school, named Saratoga Oak Street School, they find their chairs and quickly get into their own places in the Moon Boat. A note is pinned to the tree (against all rules of ecology). Who can read it? Well, I am called upon for that honour.

I take it, saying, 'I do wish someone besides myself could read'. I read the note that says, 'Every day you sit in these chairs that are made from the great oak tree. It is getting to be the end of November and I have not heard you remembering our oak tree family.'

'Remember us.' What does that mean? Then everyone says, 'Thank you, oak tree', and we hug the tree. Then we measure to see how many of us it will take to hug the tree. Yes, 'it is a four-hugger tree'. Then we sing Mia's song: 'Thank you, thank you, thank you very much', as we go in. How nice of the oak tree to remind us to say 'thank you'.

Have we forgotten to say 'thank you' to other things in the room? This is the signal to be thankful for everything in our room. The children sit by one particular thing in the room and tell their story of being thankful that it is in our Kindergarten room. And then in some wonderful mysterious way, it usually comes to some child that there are other things in the school that need to be thanked. How could we do this? Someone always says, 'Let's make a thank-you sign'.

The room begins to be filled with printed 'thank yous'. These signs spill out into the halls, down the corridors, and into the office and library. You see them pinned everywhere. I often wonder what visitors think as they enter the school and see our Kindergarten signs everywhere.

Where else can we put our thank-yous? Soon we find ourselves making many signs to take home to hide in our mother's shoe or under our daddy's pillow. The children begin to tell each other where they can hide them at home. Small 'thank you' signs are printed by the children and kept in an envelope, ready to travel home.

Parents have come to me later and told me of the pleasure these little notes have brought to them when they were discovered in their hiding places. There can never be enough thank-yous in the world.

The Mother's Lap

Every child needs a mother's lap. Since there are not enough mother's laps in the world, I decided to have one special one in the Kindergarten room. It had to be a special chair. My son, Bill, had been given an old overstuffed chair that wasn't being used, and it was exactly right for the Mother's Lap.

In early matriarchal society, the shape of the chair was moulded after the woman's body. It was the throne on which she sat. This chair I was given to use was voluptuous, with a cozy feeling when you'd sink into it. Soft and enveloping... it's everything a mother's lap should be. However, it was in such a sad condition, and not at all the right colours, that I asked Karen and Dean's mother, who was an artist, to help. She made it into a great big mother who exudes love. Her boots hang to the floor; her face shines out from the back of the chair; her arms envelop us. It is where I sit when I gather the children for story time; and this is where the children can go when they don't feel well. Then they are covered by a beautiful handmade blanket knitted by my sister, Jan. It is not uncommon to see one or two children in the Mother's Lap at one time.

When I told my neighbour, Virginia, about the Mother's Lap in the Kindergarten and how cozy it was and how it just welcomed all those who needed an extra bit of love, she said, 'Where is this mother's lap? I sometimes feel the need to sit in a mother's lap like that.'

Fairy Tales and Storytelling

The art of storytelling lies with the experience of the storyteller himself. How has he come to this story? Does it resonate in him from his childhood? Does he himself feel the wisdom and magic of this story? Does he know not to rob the children of bringing their own gifts of imagination to the tale of wonder? Does he know to speak in a dream-like way, not too full of effort and drama, but with just enough mystery in his voice to make them feel the picture of the story and that the story is just right for them? Does the world stop as we both enter into this mystical moment called story time? Can we give up ourselves and our world to take on images that live and will continue to live and enrich us forever? Is our anticipation sharpened to cut away all that is false, leaving only the purity of enchantment that releases all that we need to feed our souls?

Fortunate is the Kindergarten day that rolls itself into a cozy ball of relatedness, where the story spills over it all. The season wraps its arms around everything that the day brings, and this means that each season demands its own list of stories.

The story touches everything we do. We live within the walls of that story we hear over and over again. All our activities, number work, reading, and so on come from the heart of the story. All things are all things.

At all times there should be just enough light in the room to set the mood. Never are the overhead lights on in the Kindergarten room at any time, let alone story-time. This kind of lighting fragments the children into a thousand pieces. The children love the cosy feel that comes when we use floor lamps instead.

But what a thrill to feel how the fog needs to hide so much of the sunlight to make it feel important. How different it is from the light the rain throws on us. To feel the sudden shadow a cloud gives to us as it crosses the sun's path into our room… perhaps a candle is the best of all light for a story!

And every story somehow finds its song, poem, dance, rhythm for its Amen. Every story needs an Amen; one is not complete without the other. The mood is broken, and we are brought back to reality. The rhythmic pattern of the story and its song follow our own rhythm of breathing in and breathing out.

The life of the story is not complete without referring to others who have also loved the story. After I have told the story many times, I bring illustrated books of the story for the children to see how different illustrators brought life to the story through their artwork. We now have a chance to compare and contrast the artist's work. And because we are all artists, we will draw pictures of the story our own way. We are not cameras. I begin to draw my own pictures. I will show what came first, then a picture for the middle of the story, and one for the last part of the story. The children will watch, knowing that they will soon be doing it their own way. We record the story in our own story-books and dramatize it at the end of the week. The story flows into song, poetry, singing games, and rhythms, and deep into our hearts forever.

The wisdom of the fairy tale is needed in the everyday setting of the Kindergarten (as well as in our lives). Fairy tales are housed so beautifully in the stories from the brothers Grimm. No Kindergarten day is complete without these stories from the Grimms' tales.

There are many forms this experience of the fairy tale can take. I follow the steps of the development of language itself. The children listen to the story as the teacher tells it over and over again. The same words are told each day. On Monday the story is introduced, which I share with them from the Mother's Lap. The children are in the Moon Boat, their feet on the floor, and their hands in their laps. The curtains let just enough light in to set the mood. In Kindergarten, the mood is everything. When we start to feel the anticipation of the new story for the week, I wrap myself in a beautiful antique gold-and-silver shawl.

Jill's mother found this old shawl in an antique store and, remembering how much her daughter loved the Kindergarten stories and how much this shawl looked like me, she gave it to me as a gift and I have worn it ever since. It is my symbol of putting on the 'mantle', calling on the gods for their blessings. Then the children sing with me Margret Meyerkort's 'Mother of the Fairy Tale', adapted from the Hungarian.

As I tell the story, everyone conjures up one's own picture of the fairy tale. The teacher does not break this dream mood by looking into the eyes of the child. This reality is too harsh. This is the child's own private time when one's world comes together, touched by the magic of imagination. I encourage children to prepare themselves for this time by wrapping up in special capes and gowns. When the story is finished, there is always a song, chant, or poem that helps us move our attention to more earthy, tangible tasks and awareness.

On Wednesday I show how others have loved this story. They like to see how artists have drawn this fairy tale in story-books or pictures. I find it best to have several styles of artistic work. I comment on the details, the colour, and the materials that were used. In this way I try to link these young artists in my classroom to the illustrator.

I often hear myself saying, 'The painter loved the story. He had his paints. He has loved to paint all his life. He takes care of his paints like you do. He knew where his paper was. To be a fine artist one keeps one's things in a beautiful way. He remembers to clean the brush so it goes back in its little house all ready to come out the next day. He knows how important it is to start with a clean brush.

'All these things we are learning so that we can grow up to be fine painters and paint our favourite stories. Today I am going to draw the story my way as I tell it to you. Because we are all artists, of course we will each have our own way of drawing. All our pictures will be different.' As I tell the story, I will draw three pictures. One is for the beginning of the story – this shows that the story has begun. Then there will be one picture for the middle, then one for the end of the story.'

When one sees my pictures, it is clear that they are foundations for things to come. I start with yellow-gold for people, to show that we are all alike and have our hearts of gold. Then I dress them up, to show their work on the earth. As in the Steiner Waldorf tradition, I make vague, ethereal forms to dream into. Because children can see the basic forms and bring their own imagination to them, they feel pleased and call out how wonderful they look. I try to tell them as I go along how pleased I am and how it is my very best. Sometimes I will say, 'This isn't my best, but I will try again to make it my best drawing'.

I tell them how I am an artist and I shall make it my way. And of course they, too, are artists and I will expect them to make it their own way. They know that an artist's work is never finished and that I shall work on my illustrations while they are drawing their pictures. I want to show in my pictures the feeling of how much I love drawing them until I feel a time to stop.

My pictures are posted on the room divider that I call 'the Wall'. When I take the time to work on these pictures, the children delight in the colour and detail. It is then that I can make use of the colours that are most appropriate to the mood of the story, the season, and the moment. That same day the children will illustrate the story in their three-page books, on the cover of which I write the name of the story. They 'dress up' the letters with coloured pencils, following the forms of the letters. If some of the 'clothes' don't seem to fit, we talk about clothes and how they follow our 'body lines'.

When the letters are properly dressed, the children then dictate their own words about the illustrations in their books to adults. A space is left underneath each line of words so that when the children are ready – in the New Year, when everything is new – they may copy their words. In the old way, the teacher wrote their words and read back to them. I tell the children, 'In the new way, you will write your own words under the picture as the teacher has written them, and then you and I will read your story together'.

Still later on, the children copy their own words from another piece of paper into their own books. I use coloured pencils for writing words. When borders using the form drawing of the week have been placed around the edge of the paper, a copy of the story is placed in the back of the book to take home for the parents to read the story over and over again to their child.

Blessed is the child whose parents work closely with the teacher. To live in these stories all week is a gift money cannot buy. I find that when I tell the story to the class, I tell it in a different way when it rings in my ears from my own childhood. These stories that are full of wisdom remain with us forever; they are always with us, and they resonate within us always. I feel this when I tell the children a story that has been part of my childhood. Stories are the architecture of our lives.

Nursery Rhymes

Play is the Kindergarten child's approach into life itself. It is no different from the adult's need for wholeness. Through play the child tries on the culture; it is the child's way of learning. This means that time is also given for playing with words. Tasting them with our mouths; feeling them fly across our tongues; then explode against our teeth – they are pushed and pulled around within our mouths. And with the help of our jaws they are rocked and bounced and flung out as our lips wave and hug them goodbye.... That's what happens when English nursery rhymes fly through the air from the Kindergarten mouths.

In the beginning, the child is led into the spoken word by playing with the sounds. In Kindergarten we continue this exploration of the language by learning nursery rhymes. We follow Lewis Carroll's philosophy: 'Just take care of the words and the sounds will take care of themselves.'

No one really masters the English language unless they are versed in nursery rhymes, these little miniature fairy tales, as they are often called. Each one in itself has swept into our English literature through historical events, work, seasons, or vast cosmic impressions that still to this day nourish our growth. Nursery rhymes also make possible the chanting that gives the five-year-old delight in the security of the difficult consonant formations that become the intellectual exercise of speaking and enunciating clearly.

Rhyming – what better way to play with the English language! 'If you are going to understand anything, you have to love it', said Goethe. And so through playing with these sounds in a joyful way the door is open to our mother tongue, the English language. The discovery of rhyme for the child is no different from Helena of Troy's discovery. The Greeks had not yet come into rhyming. When Helena hears rhyming that Faust uses, Goethe has her saying to Faust:

'Manifold marvels do I see and hear.
Amazement strikes me, I would fain ask much,
But first I'd ask to know why that man's speech
Sounded so new and strange, strange and yet friendly.
It seems that one tone makes way for another,
And hath a word grown friendly to the ear,
Another woos caressingly the first.'

Later she says, 'Then tell me how to learn such lovely speech'.

We learn our 'lovely speech' through the nursery rhyme, and in the Kindergarten there is a time each week for this experience. The mood is set through ceremony that opens the child up to the nourishing feeling of expectation. Nothing is ever presented without first setting the mood.

Pictures of the nursery rhyme sit on a pedestal, waiting to be unveiled. We sing the words 'Mother Goose now comes today, bringing her dear rhymes this way' to welcome the verses. Each rhyme has its own gestures, and these dramatic gestures become a vital part of the learning, for now the whole body is involved.

At the close of the lesson, the picture of the nursery rhyme is returned to its special box with the song of Mother Goose flying away. The putting away, the coming home, is the benediction itself. Between each rhyme, while the chosen child is changing the picture, we sing:

Long ago in London Town
Mother Goose came flying down.
When we wait, we sing this song.
Right is right and wrong is wrong.'
                    bp

Later we realize that we are in need of knowing exactly how to find the nursery rhyme we need, which is placed in its own box near the Mother Goose picture.

We must not cheat the child out of making this discovery of a need for order, as though it were his own idea or invention that each rhyme has a special place of its own. As Nietzsche said, 'You must become a chaos if you would give birth to a dancing star'. Order comes out of chaos — no one knows this better than the Kindergarten teacher. How

MOTHER GOOSE SONG

Betty Peck

Long a - go in Lon-don Town,   Moth-er Goose came   fly-ing down.

When we wait, we sing this song.   Right is right and   wrong is wrong.'

can we make it easier to find and visit each nursery rhyme? How to do this is the question. All possibilities are available to them and all are tried by the Kindergarten children, but in the end, it has never failed to bring forth the words of the universal filing system: Use 'J' for Jack-Be Nimble. YES, then each rhyme has its own special alphabetical home.

Most children know nursery rhymes when they enter Kindergarten. Connecting the child to the familiar for expansion of skills that are needed is an important component of learning. Adding newness and life to what is already familiar is one of the roles of the teacher.

When it is time for drawing a picture of the rhyme, I draw a picture first, giving particular attention to detail and colour, and then the children draw theirs. These will be put into their own nursery rhyme book, accompanied by the words for the nursery rhyme. Each week's drawing for the rhyme becomes more vivid and alive than the last.

The rhymes are chosen to wrap themselves around the sound of the week (see pp. 115-116). When the letter of the week is 'W', the rhyme is 'Wee Willie Winkie.' Each week we add another rhyme to our repertoire and review others in order. After the review, the pictures are returned to their special place as we sing:

'Mother Goose now flies away, taking her dear rhymes away.'

On the day when we each take our own nursery rhyme books home, we have a Mother Goose party to which the parents are invited. When the parents arrive, they are given the Mother Goose caps that we have made.

We start the programme with the ringing of a bell that sounds the note 'A'. It is important to hear in your ear this cosmic sound that ties us in with the universe. The presentations consist of puppet shows and group or solo recitations of the rhymes. Our Mother Goose song is sung at the beginning of each presentation throughout the celebration.

After the programme, we go to the garden, where all the foods of the Mother Goose rhymes can be found at different locations, placed here in the garden by the children and their mothers. All the food for the party is from the nursery rhymes. The children have made the signs and pictures to go with each verse that has been chosen. A great deal of thought has gone into preparing what food they would bring: there are curds and whey with a spider hanging down; there are tarts set on a table near the Queen of Heart's crown; there is plum pudding, into which each child reached and got a plum on his thumb; there is pease porridge, with a sign saying, 'Pease porridge hot, pease porridge cold'. This hand-made sign stands by the two porridge pots.

Then there are Humpty Dumpty's hard-boiled eggs. Silver bells and cockle-shells are there also. There is an enlarged cut-out of a little girl, who has a little curl made of wood curlings for the nursery rhyme 'There was a little girl who had a little curl'.

The children have placed chairs somewhere in the garden for their parents. On the chairs are their beautiful hand-crafted Mother Goose book, with the drawings that the children have made of the nursery rhymes they have learned each week. Printed across from each illustration are the words of the nursery rhymes – this becomes their own illustrated, personalized Nursery Rhyme Book.

With their child, the parents now find their chairs in the garden. It is as much a surprise for the parents as for the children. It will be the first time that the children have seen this hand-made book that has been put together by the Teacher 'elves'. As the children sit in their parents' laps, they discover all their nursery-rhyme friends and are delighted to 'read' them to their parents.

When the children return to school the following week, all traces of our Mother Goose work are gone. One day in late spring, when Lady Spring arrives, she brings with her green apples and beautifully illustrated hardbound editions of Mother Goose books. Each book, one for every child, is wrapped with the promise not to peek until she leaves. When they open the gifts she has brought, they see their own nursery rhymes, the ones filled with memories of friends speaking together in rhythmic order. They hear the teacher's voice, saying them over and over again. They find themselves wanting to read them to themselves and to each other. They recall the weekly ceremonies that made it possible to now accept them as part of themselves. They sense the joy of movement that made the rhythm come alive. They can now draw out from their own imagination all the pictures they had put down on paper.

These words are alive wrapped in all their sensual pleasures, making it possible to unite them with more than just the words, to unite them now with more than what they are: they are deep into the love of their English language heritage.

However, because all things are all things, all these new Nursery Rhyme books soon plunge us into number sequencing: 'Where is Jack Be Nimble?' 'It's on page 34.' 'Where is page 34?' 'It's after 29.' 'Where is page 74?' 'You have gone too far. It is one more page.' For you see, when a child chooses her favourite nursery rhyme and calls out the page number, it is the number that becomes the vital vehicle for arriving at the right page.

And so the nursery rhymes, these ancient collections of the lives and times of our earlier ancestors, have launched us into the twenty-first century with a newness of life that will be a part of us for ever.

Discipline

The word 'discipline' is from the word 'disciple'. Disciple means to follow, to believe, and to want to learn so much that you are willing to give up all your old ways and turn to the new ways. This is what Kindergarten is all about, no less than salvation. Salvation means to me that when trouble comes, you are met by God Himself to turn from your old ways to a new way.

In the Kindergarten, the teacher leads the way. That is all there is to it. She sets the tone. Her questions carry the answers. Her commands carry strength for the child to follow through. This is why the Kindergarten teacher has to feel more than well when she comes to Kindergarten.

When a teacher stops and takes time to help a child, it is not wasted time for the other children. When she treats one child fairly, the others know they will be treated fairly. They see how important the action of one child is to the rest of the group.

What they are learning is more about the teacher than themselves. 'I know how she is going to handle me when I'm in trouble. Is she fair? Is she clear? Does she have a plan? Does she carry more than her own strength? Does she help everyone feel that they have learned from this experience not to have it happen again? Do we all know what our role is in being a member of the group? Does she dismiss us at the close of the encounter with a gesture or statement that lifts us to another realm, such as, "Sorry, Full Moon"?'

At all times the teacher should make herself clear. In our class we say, 'You make yourself clear, whether you are speaking or writing'. The teacher may have to stop and say, 'Oh, I guess I did not make myself clear. I do want to make myself clear'. Then she says what she said again, perhaps in a different way.

Of course, there are times when a child is not able to observe something correctly, or not able to listen for the instruction – so you say, 'Please sit over there so you can have a better view of how to do it'. I always say, 'Come and try again', when I think he is eager to return. Or more often than not, the child himself says, 'May I try again?'.

I want every disciplinary act to be the 'hot stove'. Can every action not carry its own seeds of discipline? What we are always looking for in the Kindergarten day is the consequence within the structure itself. And when it does occur, no words need to be spoken. Cause and effect have proven themselves.

When I was learning to drive, my husband said, 'Always drive five cars ahead'. I have found this to be true with children. We teachers need to teach five processes ahead. The teacher paves the way, and she set the limits. When I see them climbing the redwood tree for the first time, I say, 'When your father is standing here where I am standing, you may climb to the top of the redwood tree; but while I am here you can only climb as far as my hands will reach'.

I find that, over the years, most of the time I've never set the limits until they are needed. Sometimes this is when we see danger coming. Sometimes it has been when danger has already struck. Sometimes the tale that is handed down about some historic happening strikes terror in the heart, and often immediately, limits are set by the children themselves.

I do not believe in overprotecting the child; rather, I believe in leaving her to herself. I'm too busy-busy working in the garden. Let her get down from the wisteria vine tree herself!... Yet I also have one eye on the child who is climbing on the wisteria vine – can she solve this problem of getting down safely? I want her to try to solve it herself. If a child is overprotected, she will grow to be nervous, to lack concentration, and to have basic insecurities. What discoveries will this child make in getting down by herself?

I try to keep busy in the garden with one eye on the children. I want them to feel free to try on the world, to make mistakes, to try out their ideas. Kindergarten is the place to discover what you are all about at five years old. It is a time to build your strength, both inner and outer.

The Latin word education is 'to lead'. The child is led, guided, by the teacher. It is the teacher's example of her own self-discipline that sets the tone for the class. She shows how we are all in this together. Her needs and the child's needs must be met; it is like the trees depending on us for our breath of carbon dioxide and us depending on them for our breath of oxygen. The teacher says, 'How beautiful the room looks when the rainbow of colour shines, knowing all its bits of colour are home safe'. All the crayons, coloured pencils, honey crayons, and water paints are kept under the rainbow. Dyed cheesecloth of rainbow colours hangs from the top of the structure that houses all our colour-making materials, plus our rainbow-coloured towels. Orderliness is an important part of discipline. Therefore the teacher sets up the room with this in mind, so that everyone knows where the crayons belong.

The teacher's need for order matches the children's need for order. They will know where to find the crayons, as the teacher needs to find crayons for her work. I say to the children that the crayons have no wings or feet of their own; they need you to lift them back to their home. Or I will say, 'Your coat is crying on the floor....Your plate is crying on the floor'. If you work through fantasy, which is the child's world, the child will respond with willingness. 'Pick them up because I say so' has little meaning to his need to rescue the situation. But when you speak his language, the language he knows, he will be glad to stop his plate from crying on the floor.

I find that many situations can be forestalled by a story, and I have often tried putting their problems into a story, using animals in some way to mirror their situation. If a child continues to play with sticks, I begin: 'Mother Bear told her Little Bear never to run with a stick in his hand. But little Baby Bear did not obey his mother and ran down the hill with his stick. He fell and the stick ran right through his head. "That's all right", said Mother Bear to Daddy Bear. "You take one side of the stick and I'll take the other, and we can carry him home where he will be safe."' The story always ends with an amusing situation that causes laughter to take over the healing of the problem.

If I see that a little girl needs to enter a play situation with others and is not being allowed to, I sit down with them and tell them a story filled with hope and expectation about a Fairy Queen who flies near gardens, hoping to put her golden fairy dust on her favourite number of children playing together. 'And I've heard it said that the one who is the kindest of all in the group sometimes sprouts fairy wings!' These stories are told spontaneously on the spot – and then off they go to play, with their feet rooted in their world of fantasy.

There should be no punishment or reward. Punishment removes the child from responsibility. It is reward enough that he has a feeling of great worth when his work is well done. He knows when he has done his best. I might say, 'How proud you must be of that straight "T"'. Rewards only come from God.

The teacher does not sit as the great judge, saying 'This is good and this bad'. It is her duty to enable the child to evaluate her own worth. You want them to be responsible: you want them to hear the spilled milk crying out for a sponge, not words that would bring a loss of dignity to the one who spilled the milk; you want the torn paper to cry for the tape, not a cry to embarrass the child who tore the paper; you want the singing game to cry out for a strong heartbeat, and so on. I feel it important to pay no attention to these slip-ups.

Everything should be handled by a *creative discipline of love* that leads the child into physical health and adulthood. However, a child needs a brick wall to kick against and feel the strength of the castle that protects him. This is certainly true through adolescence.

When children find it hard to settle in, I say:

'When you sit, you sit.

When you stand, you stand.

You don't wobble about!'

I often hear the children saying this to each other.

'While we wait, we sing this song: Right is right, and wrong is wrong.' I have often sung this when we are going from one activity to another, and we find our Mother Goose Rhymes waiting for us to begin the next activity. But better still and most effective is the positive element brought to everyone's attention:

'Well, it must be May! Look at all of you telling me you are ready.'

'Look how the golden ring sparkles and shines over there.'

'Look how straight Brian stands.'

'Oh, what a beautiful thank you.'

'Gold is falling from Phoebe's mouth.' (Referring to the story of 'The Three Little Men in the Woods')

What I find most effective is talking over their heads to the other teacher and saying, 'Mrs Dooley, did you hear that?'. Then the child repeats his special thank-you or idea. 'Mrs Dooley, you are going to be so pleased when you hear this news!'

Is it strange that my thoughts on discipline have now become the subject of building the child's ego, his positive feelings about himself? Calling a child's attention to his great discovery puts his thought on a pedestal and crowns it with glory. 'Mrs Dooley, wait until you hear David's idea....' There is the yin and yang in everything; therefore we cannot talk about discipline without talking about self-esteem.

I try never to say a 'no' without a 'yes'. 'Yes, you may do that, but not now. We are going for a walk', and so on. 'Yes, you may have a cookie, but not now. The ice cream is ready.' I learned this long ago with my own two children.

I never call children to me unless I have something important for them to do. When I see that a child needs a change of space, I say sternly, 'John, come here'. Then I say just as sternly, 'I need you, John'. Then I send him on an errand or give him some important job. I want the children to trust my strong voice of authority. I want them to have trusted me over and over again, so that if the day comes when they must move quickly because of danger, they know that it is important to move at once.

Authority comes from the root word 'author'. We are the authors of the direction we want our lives to take, and that includes the Kindergarten class. We are in charge as teachers. I call those who help me 'Little Teachers'. They are not the teacher, but I want them to feel their rightful roles, responsible to themselves and each other. So I say, 'Heather, would you be the Little Teacher today and take my place at the Silver Sea?'. Or I say, 'You are just like a Little Teacher' when I want to call attention to someone's worth.

I have learned over the years never to 'talk into a storm'. The teacher must somehow distract the child to bring her into another focus when she is overburdened with the moment. She can call for the healing basket, or say, 'Oh, I do believe you will need Band-Aids and we haven't one left. Please choose a friend and go to the office and get some.' This has broken up many fits of sobbing. Or I say, 'Come, show me where it happened. Where was he standing? Where were you standing? Show me how it happened.' Or I rush to get blankets to wrap him in. Then he stays in his little cocoon until he bursts forth new again.

When a child comes and tells me some long tale about being bothered by another child, I say very seriously, 'Thank you for telling me'. This shows respect for her confidence in me. It also closes the door on that situation so that the child can feel free to start playing again, knowing that she has done her part in reporting, and that now the gods will take over. She has cast her bread upon the water.

The teacher sets the pattern for handling problems. She teaches the child to handle his own problems – which can be done in several ways. We often do this by role-playing. Learning to make himself clear, the child says to the other child who is causing his trouble, 'I do not like what you're doing. Stop it.' Or, 'Stop, you are hurting me and I do not like it'.

I also call attention to someone's action and say, 'You see, don't you, why everyone wants to play with Bryce? Did you see how kind he was to his friend, Eric?' The teacher constantly points out helpful behaviour to the class or group. She constantly calls attention to ways children are polite to each other and to her. She constantly points out children who help with the daily work. All of this helps the children in their skills of friendship, which is the outcome of thoughtfulness, kindness, and caring.

When it is full moon, Kindergartens all over the country go down the drain. One has no control at all over this psychic phenomenon. The moon that controls the planetary waters somehow considers our water supply within our own human bodies as part of its realm! And so we are all literally drawn right out of our skin. In some sense we seem to be in no way different from the tides of the shore.

How does one cope with this with twenty little ones all feeling 'high'? I have learned to have a special routine, which helps sometimes more than other times. Routine, perhaps, is the answer.... We plan the celebration of the 'Full Moon'. This consists of first making moon books. We have a special moon poem. We write in a book that has been prepared for us out of black night skies with a drooping moon with silver sailing by. We dress like the moon. We have a special moon cape of silver and a silver moon crown. If more than one child wants to be the moon, he can be one of Jupiter's moons, and so on. Never is the teacher at a loss to include everyone's passion for a dramatic role.

In our Kindergarten we have all been amazed at the little moon that wanders into our room on full-moon days and sits on our walls. Even in May of 1988, two moons came to dance on the walls. This was the month that gave us two full moons. We are always delighted to see them. And I feel that with the children it is perfectly natural and to be expected. But secretly, Mrs. Dooley, my aid, and I look at each other and wonder why: Why is it possible to have this small, round, dancing light come to our Kindergarten? It will even dance to the rhythm of our poem. Why so faithful to its scheduled sky appearance? Why do we expect our Kindergarten moon to shine on our walls at this special time? Is this happening to other Kindergartens, who chart the moon each day and who know the calendar is written in the sky? So you see, full-moons are very real to us in more ways than one.

We also plan extra playtime. We fill up two rain barrels of water that can be used that day. Normally we use only one rain barrel full of water a day. This has always seemed a needed control – for both plants and growing children. But on full-moon, everything is different. We blow bubbles in a different way on full moon; they must be blown from different moon pipes that I have collected. At other times, we blow bubbles using a straw. They tumble out over the container, bumping into each other.

We take our water birds outside and fill the garden with bird song. Otherwise, they are used only on our walks through the garden, saying 'hello' to the new flowers the children have discovered. We try to have water play everywhere. Children can be seen vigorously washing clothes.

Everything is wild to match the day, and the children are caught up in moon glow without knowing that it is understood by adults that all the world is responding to the pull of moon, but never so much as in

Kindergarten. And so it is with the full moon for this Kindergarten teacher is driving five cars ahead.

One often asks me why I have so much patience with children. It isn't that I have a good deal of patience, but that from my experiences with children I know what to expect. If you understand the psychological reasons that are causing a certain behaviour, you know you are safe in letting it ride itself out. However, you stand nearby and busy yourself in the work of the garden. A teacher knows how and when to give permission to the child to solve her own problems. She does this in a clear-cut way, by keeping out of this encounter when the child is dealing with her own inner teacher.

When a parent puts her trust in a teacher and knows it is the best place for her child, then there is an unspoken authoritarianism that puts things in order. But if it's the other way around, and parents feel a loss of respect for the teacher, the burden on the child is too great and the parent should find another teacher. It is my experience that there is a right situation for every child. As teachers, we are responsible for saying when we feel we do not have the skills to deal with a child who has been damaged beyond our ability to help. There are others who have the answers, and every effort should be made to make the change to the right environment for the child. We are not gods, and in no way can we solve every problem. I have my own feet of clay, and it is important to acknowledge this from the beginning before the need to do so arises.

Discipline plays a great part in not only the parent's attitude, but in the class size. No Kindergarten should have over 20 children. It has been my experience that it is asking too much from five-year-olds to know more than 20 children at a time. It is the role of the teacher to knit the class into one big family. She sees to it that everyone is a best friend to someone in the class. She sees that children play together after school. You are a true friend if you have been invited to someone's house and you have shared some out-of-school/Kindergarten time with other members of the class.

And I mean 20 children with two teachers. The ideal is to have an apprentice teacher with a credential. Then you have a built-in substitute, should the need arise. She knows what the next steps are, and no time is lost. I speak from experience, and know this to be the ideal situation.

Furthermore, I advocate that being an assistant in a Kindergarten is how Kindergarten teachers should be trained. 'Working with the action' every day opens up all opportunities of learning. You learn why, when, where, what, and who all at once. This is integration at its best. The resident teacher is able to show the importance of the flow of the year, which is built upon week after week. An apprenticeship should last for one year. The teacher knows that it is the look in her eye and the tone of her voice that constitute materials for the first lessons to be learned in Kindergarten. The children first learn to 'read' the teacher.

What does the teacher bring to this moment of discipline? She brings years of searching, studying every path that speaks to her soul. She experiences all that she can glean from herself, her surroundings, her travels, her studies, to know who she is and what her gifts are. She is constantly changing, unfolding into new light and new understanding, and struggling to put these new learnings into practice.

Because of these experiences that have shaped my life, I feel free to let the child have time to explore his world, make his mistakes, and skin his knees. I know that this is the most vital way of learning your own direction on the path of life. It certainly has been mine. But most of us need encouragement along the way. I have the door in my Magic Cupboard for this. When children forget how wonderful they are, I open the door to the Magic Cupboard and stand them in front of the mirror that is on the other side of the door, and say, 'How could you forget how wonderful you are?'. They look at themselves in the mirror and melt. The inscription over the door says, 'THANK YOU FOR EVERY MAGIC MOMENT THAT MAKES IT POSSIBLE FOR ME TO STAND HERE AND FEEL HOW WONDERFUL I AM'. One doesn't read this to the child, for looking into the mirror is enough for them to see how truly wonderful they are. But for the adult, we must always remember it had taken 15 billion years for us to reach this moment.

How grateful we are for all these magic moments, even in our own lifetime, that have made this moment possible. It is almost impossible to comprehend how truly wonderful we are, but a time each day should be set aside in pure gratitude for this gift of life that has been entrusted to us.

eeting the Developmental Needs of the Kindergarten Child

I conclude Part I with my 'check-list' for an integrated, aesthetic programme for a Living Kindergarten:

The Teacher

The teacher:

♦ Understands the value of beauty in herself, the environment, and in all her teachings.
♦ Knows the value of bringing a positive attitude that includes a playful, cheerful tone to the Kindergarten.
♦ Knows how important the quality of her voice is in the presentation of music, poetry, and stories.
♦ Works with an understanding of the development of the child.
♦ Presents herself in an artistic way, through gestures, dress, and voice.
♦ Displays confidence and knowledge in communicating her programme that is in tune with the development of the child.
♦ Displays skill in dealing with parents' needs.
♦ Educates her colleagues, parents and the administration on the value of her integrated, aesthetic Kindergarten programme that meets the developmental needs of the child.
♦ Knows how to be renewed both professionally and personally; and spiritually
♦ Presents her integrated programme artistically.

The Environment

In the environment:

♦ There is a harmonious hum in the room.
♦ The senses are refined and nourished rather than being overloaded.
♦ There are different moods created throughout the day to facilitate learning.
♦ Natural materials are used throughout the room.
♦ There is a reverence and feeling of awe and gratitude for the gift of

the natural materials – for instance, the gift of wool from the sheep or the wood from the tree for the chairs.
♦ The furniture is easily moved to create new learning areas.
♦ Natural light is used in the room.
♦ Colour in the room acknowledges the seasons.
♦ There is a place in the room to celebrate and give thanks to Mother Earth, the sun, moon, and stars for their gifts to us in each changing season (indoor garden). Scientific observation is centred here. Materials collected by the children to use in their number work and music are visible.
♦ Flowers of the season are displayed within the child's reach.
♦ There is room for gathering together in a circle (golden ring).
♦ The outdoor play area is truly a children's garden.
♦ The children are happy to be both inside and outside.
♦ There is a seasonal fragrance to the room.
♦ The adults in the room are models worthy of imitation.

The 'Curriculum'

Play:
♦ The play material calls forth the child's imagination.
♦ There are capes and crowns to help them in their feeling of royalty.
♦ The child is able to move and create his own areas of play.
♦ There are long periods of social play planned during the day.
♦ The teacher understands the need for play and helps to facilitate it.

Language:
♦ Relaxed conversation is encouraged.
♦ There are attractive materials for writing.
♦ There is evidence that children are writing: signs posted, 'I love you' notes etc.
♦ The stories told to the children are appropriate to their age, to the season, and to the special needs of the class.
♦ Poetry and song flow from the teacher's heart.
♦ The teacher speaks in a picturesque way in order to enrich the child's imagination.
♦ The letters of the alphabet are presented through pictorial development and celebrated in meaningful ways.

- Childhood Mother Goose rhymes are honoured for their many ways of relating the child to her world.
- Seasonal programmes are presented by the children for the parents.

Drama:
- Time is given to dramatize the stories.
- The dramatizations are in the child's own words.
- There is an artistic beginning and ending to each performance.

Rhythm:
- The rhythm of the day is noticeable.
- The rhythm of the week is meaningful to the child.
- The rhythm of the year is anticipated by the child.
- An understanding of the importance of rhythm is a part of each discipline.
- The child feels secure and flows with the rhythms within the classroom.
- Birthdays are celebrated with an artistic awareness.

Music:
- Singing games are enjoyed by the teacher and child.
- Music is the thread that ties the day together: morning song, transitions, songs for work, greetings, thank-yous, good-bye.

Arithmetic:
- The child feels the rhythmic patterns of numbers.
- Discovery learning is encouraged.
- The child is invited to experience arithmetic in the world around him, through cooking, the garden, and through his own body.
- Available are the arithmetic tools and manipulative opportunities that are a part of the child's everyday life.

Science:
- The scientific disciplines of observation, classifying, comparing, recording, and predicting are part of the day's activities.
- Science is woven into the seasonal activities.
- Scientific observation is enriched by field trips to nearby gardens and farms.

PART II

The Play Garden

The Garden in the Kindergarten

Garden Day

The garden is the birthright of every child. I believe that a garden holds all the answers to life, for all of the wisdom we need is present there. In my Kindergarten teaching, I long ago discovered the need for the five year old to be in a garden. I would not teach Kindergarten without a door opening out into a garden. Friedrich Froebel coined the word Kindergarten in 1840 because he knew the combination of gardens and children is vital to the development of the human being.

Joel and Sarah's mother knew how much we loved the garden, and being an artist, she put her love into a beautiful stained glass window that shows us all in the garden. We hung it in our eastern windows in the Kindergarten room and sang this song each day.

THE GLASS IS IN THE WINDOW

To the tune of 'Coo-coo'   Words by Betty Peck

The   glass is in the   win - dow The pic-ture is of   me.   I

know I'm in the   gar - den, The garden's in - side of   me.

The glass is in the window
The picture is of me.
I know I'm in the garden,
The garden's inside of me.

TREES

I need you, said the tree, to laugh and sing and talk with me
And to walk close to me
And sit under my stretched-out arms
And be a friend to me.
To lean against me
And know that I am your special gift…
Breathe deeply and know my gift to you
As you give yours to me.

                              bp

Kindergarten Play Gardens

Play is essential to the life of the Kindergarten child. The garden is not only the richest setting for play, but it holds in secret all of life's lessons to be discovered by the child. It truly is the source of wisdom and the basis of all art. Paul Klee said, 'To penetrate to the secret place where primeval power nurtures all evolution... who is the artist that would not dwell there in the womb of nature at the source of creation where the secret key lies guarded?'.

Important Landmarks in the Kindergarten Play Garden

Play Structures
The first year we moved into our Kindergarten, a pine-plank wooden form called 'The Structure' was built in our large sandbox. The name gave the children permission to make it into anything their imagination dictated – a ship, a house, a train. The feeling of power comes over young children when they stand above the teacher, above his fellow students, above growing plants. It allows them to stand nearer the sky, the sun, the stars, the moon, and their dreams. The place was made larger and more secretive when a parent planted two aromatic pine trees there, on either side, guarding the entrance.

The Garden Gate
The importance of the garden gate should not be overlooked. The need to 'enter into...' establishes a separation between what is and what could be. The child needs boundaries, as well as a beginning and ending, thereby establishing permission to begin anew. The child leaves the outside world and enters into his own world; and the opportunity for the sense of anticipation to form strong roots at this age makes possible a lifetime of joy. Entering the garden gate brings with it a sense of anticipation as though one is entering a secret garden that holds unknown adventures.

Rain Barrel
I always keep a traditional rain barrel in the garden and make sure it's filled up with water every day. I refer to all water as 'rainwater'. Not only is water used for play by the children but the ritual of drinking

rainwater helps our children learn to receive water in gratitude. The cycle of the raindrop's life becomes a vital part of their learning. Their 'thank yous' fill the air when they realize that no drop of water is ever lost. When they turn on the tap, or dip water out of our rain barrel, I want them to picture all that has happened to provide them with what is now theirs to drink and to play with.

To capture the rain is something a child can experience as caretakers of Planet Earth. To be able to express gratitude to all who help capture the raindrops, sending this water to us to use, gives the child the opportunity to feel connected to the great forces of life. When they turn on the water, the picture of all that has gone into providing them with this rainwater is now theirs and their 'thank yous' again fill the air.

Not only is water used for play, but the ritual of drinking the rainwater is afforded great importance – accompanied by song, pitchers and cups, tickets, and good manners.

Sand

Sand holds endless possibilities for the development of the imagination. The building and rebuilding of everything that has been a part of their lives is a vital part of sand play. Re-creating the world is indeed the work of childhood. Sand belongs in the garden for many reasons – one being that it forms the great waterways of the world in our sand play. The rivers, lakes, streams, and oceans must be re-created, giving opportunity to understand the property of sand, water, rocks, and wood.

As you know, I would not have taken the Kindergarten job at Saratoga School on Oak Street unless my Kindergarten door opened into a garden. So I found myself designing an ideal garden when the answer was, yes, I could have the Kindergarten door open into a garden.

The first thing to be built was the sandbox. This was bordered by 12-inch edging that we could use to sit on or use in many ways with our play. A climbing structure was placed in the middle of the sandbox. When the children arrived we had everything but the sand itself.

So when they saw that there was no sand, they said, 'Where is the sand?'. 'Oh', I said, 'Yes, we have no sand, I wonder how sand is made? Have you ever felt sand?' 'Oh yes', they said. 'How does it feel? Are those little grains hard or soft? What is the hardest thing you know?' When someone said, rock', I picked up a rock and said, 'Is it possible to make sand out of this rock? What do I need?' Then someone said, 'Let's get two rocks and rub them together'. And so for days we made sand – small pieces falling on our clothes day after day. Then after school, word came that our sand was to be delivered over the weekend. 'No, we are making are own sand. However, you may drive slowly by at 10.30 in the morning and perhaps we will see you and be ready for your truck-load of sand.' And so, as we were rubbing our rocks together, someone saw this slow-moving truck full of sand. It became ours. Never cheat the child out of taking the first steps into experiencing life on every level.

Structures

The garden is a place for having raised platforms made of wood. Children need to feel themselves to be off the ground; a feeling of power comes to a five-year-old when she stands above the teacher, above her fellow students, above the growing plants. But more important still is that it is here she stands nearer the sky, the sun, the stars, the moon – and her dreams. If the structure has no name, it can be a ship, a house, a spaceship, or whatever. Climbing is fundamental to childhood.

Paths

The need for processions through the garden to celebrate all the activities of the day means that having paths throughout the garden becomes a necessity. They are always a wheelbarrow's width wide and, if possible, the paths are lined with fragrant plants, such as lavender, so that all the senses can be fed at once. Children prepare for these processionals along the garden paths in many imaginative ways by making banners, costumes, and so on.

Swing

From 'The Structure' hangs the garden swing. The children's need to spin – vestibular stimulation – was at first satisfied by an old tyre large enough to hold three children at the same time. I could not find a better spinning form than this until I found a hammock-like Australian model that swung low to the ground and comfortably held two children and their teacher. These swings, holding two children as well as the teacher as they do, are low to the ground. They can be attached to any hook and taken inside.

Moveable Equipment

Logs and stumps as well as large rocks, tables, and benches are engineered around the garden through cooperative team effort. The experience of building with this kind of equipment provides meaningful play on all levels of learning.

Planter Boxes

Planter boxes provide benches by framing them with 2-by-6 inch boards. Twelve inches high is suggested for large planting area boxes. This makes it easier for the teacher and child to be at a convenient level for observation of the miracle of plant life, and provides built-in benches. Small paths can be made within the large planter boxes.

Compost Pile

Compost is the gold of the garden; it is here that the child observes life into death and death into life, and it is therefore centrally located in the Kindergarten Garden. Every leaf of the deciduous trees is claimed by the Kindergarten. All cookie crumbs from the class are put into the 'Return to the Earth Bucket' inside the classroom. When it is full, it is carried out majestically by the children to place on the compost.

Children collect egg-shells and crush them into food for the soil. There is never enough real work for children to do. Rabbit droppings, along with pony and horse manure, are brought in by parents, neighbours, and friends for the compost. 'All things are all things' is an important message of the compost. During the spring the compost is distributed to the garden in great ceremony. Pumpkin seeds can be planted in the compost and left to grow over the summer months.

Dancing Green

A 'dancing green' gives many hours of enjoyment, not the least being the use of a daisy lawn mix that is the source of many charming daisy chains. May Day dancing on a circle of green around the Maypole is one of the many celebrations of Spring. Because singing games are a vital part of the everyday celebration of life in the Kindergarten, a 'dancing green' is needed in the garden.

Bird Bath

If possible a bird bath should be a part of every garden. The responsibility of keeping it clean and filled is part of the plan to incorporate real work. In addition to real work it welcomes the birds and gives us all a chance to participate in caring for small creatures around us.

These necessary areas of importance which we call 'landmarks' in a Children's Play Garden invite the child into the world of the garden, which is his home.

An Environment for Outdoor Play

When some of the eucalyptus trees were taken down in the schoolyard, I pleaded for the wood from these great giants to be used for play equipment. Where else could one find such an experience of beauty to feel, climb, and smell, that had been sculptured by the sun, rain, and wind for our pure enjoyment? I soon found myself reduced to begging for just a few logs from the limbs. 'Too dangerous', Henry, our beloved custodian said. 'I stand for danger', I responded, as I stood there marking the ones I wanted. A few were rolled over to our Kindergarten. One large log that I would not give up was finally brought over and placed in our garden. This log was in the shape of a cradle. Here on this spot – Saratoga Oak Street School – I wanted them to experience again the cradle of our known civilization. This wood was from the trees that stood here when the first school was built on this property. The Kindergarten holds within it the beginning roots of our public school system. The 'rocking' of the cradle, which is the responsibility of the teacher's hand, must touch all. That hand must contain the finest that humankind offers, including the most up-to-date knowledge that enhances the ancient wisdom that flows out to cradle the newness of tomorrow.

Would that every Kindergarten were blessed with this symbolism, cut from wood from a nearby fallen tree.

I now have apple trees planted around the cradle; perhaps we could have chosen birch, but I chose apple because of its five-ness. Its blossoms, its fruits, its life-cycle of dying into new life, its fragrance, its invitation to the bees, its legendary qualities in our literature, and in its heart, the form of a five-pointed star when we cut it in half that tells us that Christmas will come again. This was the only sunny place in our garden where apple trees would grow.

I remember when they were replacing the telephone pole across the street. I ran over and said, 'Please, could you cut the old pole up into twelve-inch pieces for us to use in the Kindergarten?'. These logs are now used in our Kindergarten as seats in our indoor garden. Money can't buy this kind of much-needed equipment.

We now have large logs in our garden, given by friends who have logged on their own property – these are wonderful for the children to move about. Children need to design their own space. My experience has been that when a formal playhouse is set up, it robs the children of exploring the possibilities of building their own. Of course, the logs are dangerous, but that is life. And unless the child is rooted in real-life experience, she will not be in command of her own courage as an adult. It is the job of the teacher to keep out of her way, while watching out of the corner of her eye for the overall safety of the situation.

I believe in discoveries; it is damaging for the child to be given rules that lock him into a situation, rules that are not his own rules. It is better to have meaningful rules that we can point to and say, 'This is John's discovery. Remember when someone left a log on the path, and he fell over it'.

Every Kindergarten makes Indian tepees. I have tried many kinds, but the ones that have proved the most valuable are the ones Nancy made for our Kindergarten. The children can move their Indian camps from place to place – which, of course, was the pattern of the Indian tribes. These tepees are by far the best – we have four of them that are decorated with Indian designs. Playground equipment needs to include jump ropes and hoops for Spring, and chalk for drawing a hopscotch pattern. I see so many play areas with this already painted on. The joy of making your own cannot be compared to a life-less adult design. And who wants to see a hopscotch when you are an Indian?

Of course, the main concern about a play area for the children is their need for different levels appropriate to facilitating their 'growing up.' The very same year we moved into our Kindergarten, all the parents helped to build a two-storey structure that has always been called 'the Structure'… a name which gives them permission to make it into anything their imagination dictates. It has been made larger and more secretive by Andreas's mother, who planted two pine trees on either side. The wood used in the construction is pine. Never does one forget the importance of tying the world together in family groups.

The structure with its swing is bedded into a large sandbox. This sand area is edged with a wide wooden border that becomes a bench which I use to gather children together. The children use it in many ways, such as for making cookies in their cooking kitchen. I can't say enough for sand. It is truly one of the tools of the gods for the Kindergarten child. Another gift of the gods is water. With our rain barrel filled with water to use each day, real metal buckets are used to provide our water supply anywhere in the garden. The best of all play equipment is sand, rock, and water.

I could not teach without a garden outside the door of the Kindergarten room. Every child I know has delighted at the secret spaces the garden holds and in finding a place to build her house with the outdoor cloths that become walls, curtains, beds, and so on.

A garden is always in need of a large table, a table where we can all work on our clay projects; a table that we can decorate for special occasions; a table where we all gather to break bread together. We put our table near our tall redwood tree. This made it possible for the redwood tree and the table to have many wonderful conversations, for this table was made of redwood long ago by Meg's father.

The garden has a 'garden house' that was made of lath, with wisteria over the top. It has been used in dramatic plays, Mother's Day celebrations, and in many other imaginative ways. We also wait on the benches for our mothers to pick us up when our day is over.

Mrs Dooley, my assistant, takes her basket of necessities out with her into the garden – holding as it does yarn, scissors, paper and pencil for sign-making, clothespegs, and so on. Materials are controlled and yet free for the asking. And soon everything is being tied up, signs are being made, and playtime is a hive of activity. Playtime must be the involvement in the deepest sense: with each other, involvement with the earth, involvement with the equipment, involvement with ideas, with their imagination and discoveries.

We have a large compost area which one can climb upon and then look in, or just dance around it. It is one of our beauty spots in the garden.

Part III

The Kindergarten Classroom

Arranging the Classroom

As I research the link between our inner states and our external environment, I find the importance of harmonizing people and places is often overlooked in our schools.

If there is a door in the room that is not used, or the children are not allowed to use, I place a mirror on the door at their eye level to help them feel included in the whole room.

In order to create a sense of well-being for everyone, I ask parents to bring fresh flowers each week that are appropriate for each season. Beautiful seasonal bouquets and indoor gardens that are visible from every part of the room provide a life-giving centre for beauty.

I trust my intuition and always keep glaring overhead lights off in my Kindergarten room. Instead, I use lamps that set the mood on grey days with a soft glow. I believe that electronic currents influence young children. The electro-magnetic field in and around the classroom can be evaluated, such as overhead lights, floor covering, and appliances. This makes it possible for these areas to be avoided in setting up the room.

I create a centre of beauty to be seen on entering the classroom. In my Kindergarten I also have many lesser centres of interest, but just as beautiful. One of the areas is set aside for our Mother Goose, where we say her rhymes and keep the drawings and other materials that enrich this important activity. This important area is always near where we gather to celebrate the letter of the week.

The indoor garden is the setting to celebrate the days of our year. It is here in the indoor garden that we celebrate not only our birthdays, holidays, and special events but also the phases of the moon. The colourful calendars in our room, which I sometimes call the Birthday boards, open the life force of time.

To increase children's sense of anticipation, I drape a lovely piece of silk over charts in my classroom, to unveil at appropriate times. I like to honour Father Sun and Mother Earth every day in my classroom. I suspend splendid stars from the ceiling of my room. Crystals catch the sunlight and vitalize the classroom with rainbow dances on sunny days.

On the warmly painted empty walls in a classroom dance the dreams of the child. One or two very inspiring pictures can be hung at the eye level of the children. I have walked into many a classroom that gave me an overpowering feeling of distraction. Every inch of the four walls was cluttered. There was no focus in the room, and therefore the children and teachers were continuously challenged to find clarity in their thoughts and feelings. I place children's art in the halls of the school, not in the classrooms.

Nothing is more demeaning to the eye than to have the colours of the rainbow presented without imagination or beauty. Iris was the Greek name for the goddess of the rainbow. Each teacher in her own creative way, like the goddess Iris, can present the colours of the rainbow to bring order to the lives of Kindergarten children. This colourful expression of the lawful universe is essential to the development of the child. I hang our dress-up capes in rainbow order. The crayons and paint are in rainbow order. The children delight in this orderly gift of the universe.

I do not allow synthetic and plastic materials in my Kindergarten. Everything is made entirely of natural materials. Children who are given the gift of furniture made of wood receive life forces of the tree to soothe and build their inner lives. Caring for this gift awakens respect for the furniture and a beginning realization that we are one with the earth. Families or organizations might contribute a chair or table with a brass label marked with the donor's name.

To establish a feeling of family and togetherness, we sit in the 'golden ring' in the centre of the room. If a child is absent, a star is drawn in their place and we sing, 'We'll make a star for David for all the world to see. We'll make a star for David until he comes back to me.'

WE'LL MAKE A STAR FOR DAVID

Betty Peck

We'll make a star for Da-vid   for all the world to see.

We'll make a star for Da-vid   un - til he comes back to   me.

When I have to deal with a difficulty, I sit in a high-back chair of authority. My desk is not a part of the Kindergarten decor because the teacher's place of power is everywhere in the Kindergarten. Instead, I position special chairs as my thrones, decorated with care, in the room and garden, with small upright logs or tables next to the chairs on which to place needed material.

I often bring objects into the classroom that evoke memories of my own days of childhood. These cherished gifts give the classroom a tangible sense of generations of continuity.

Fragrance in the Kindergarten Room

The fragrance that wafts from the Kindergarten room on bread-making day brings the whole school to our door. This happens again and again every Wednesday, the day we bake our cookies, which we shape into the form of the 'letter of the week'. Every Thursday we bake bread.

During the winter months, I burn incense in the room. Arturo, one of the student teachers in our school, stopped by our room. 'It's like going into a temple, the lights are low, there is the smell of incense. I could hardly find the teacher', he said to the faculty. This ground is sacred, and five-year-olds are here, newborn to the earth and to the halls of learning.

This heavy smell of the woods is sometimes combined with the smell of pine needles from our pine tree. We rub the pine needles on all the furniture in the room. Sometimes the redwood cones are put in the oven to make the room fragrant. We also do this with eucalyptus. We fill a pot with spices and heat it in the oven. We bake the spices during the first week in January. We fill the room with the aroma of cinnamon, cloves, and nutmeg. This continues off and on through St. Valentine's Day.

The harvest of autumn brings its own smells of apples, sage, peppermint leaves, and eucalyptus pods. We take these pods and put them into hand-sewn bags. These are given to people to wear around their necks if they have colds.

We fill hearts full of lavender from the garden. I am always thinking of ways of getting more fragrance into the lives of Kindergarten children. I find that fragrance association is very strong, and I wish to capitalize on it for grounding their experiences into total saturation of the senses.

Our counting sticks are made of lemon wood – we make them ourselves. We take the leaves off and trim the sticks.

Our neighbours and friends add to our supply of rose petals for our Mother's Day gifts. This fragrance in our room is enjoyed by all. Then comes the day we make special containers for all the rose petals, to be turned into gifts. I always have baskets of 'good smells' around the room. Flower petals with spices are one of them. We are always aware of the fragrance of everything that grows in our garden.

When the first Spring rain comes, we dash outside to drink in its beauty. I don't want them to miss out on the joy of revitalizing themselves through the smells and fragrances that Mother Earth provides.

The Tables

In Kindergarten the gathering of the class at one large table provides a setting needed to establish a feeling of community. It is here we all break bread together. A smaller table in addition to the large one is used on feast days to arrange the food, thus helping to develop many skills such as serving, decorating, counting, and planning.

When these tables are not being used to hold the gifts from the garden we call food, there is no end of the possibilities in which they can be used. They become props for the child's imagination.

Tips for the Kindergarten from Feng Shui

In recent years I have trained professionally in Feng Shui and add this to my previous knowledge. I enjoy bringing balance into the space for the child's and the teacher's creative work. To call forth clear vision, the Feng Shui practitioners hang a brass chime just inside the schoolroom door. We learn in this Art of Placement that straight lines attract negative energy. To help counteract sharp corners, straight rows, and hard edges, one can soften and bring a feeling of welcoming arms to a room. The flow of chi in the teacher is as important as it is in the classroom itself. Young children can be negatively influenced by split views, angled or blocked walls, or slanted ceilings. There is always a cure to help balance imperfection of shapes.

The art of Feng Shui is used outside in the garden as well as inside the classroom. A large sitting stone brings a feeling of stability to the children's outdoor play area. If the outdoor classroom is near a busy street or corridor, a moving form such as a windmill, whirligig, or weather vane can stimulate chi and ward off overbearing influences. A mobile can also be used inside the room.

Here are some other ways to use Feng Shui:

1. Classrooms feel the pressure of low ceilings; there is no buoyancy, no light-heartedness, no joy. Practitioners who have worked with Feng Shui feel that putting bamboo poles in each of the four corners from floor to ceiling gives a lift to the spirit. Bamboo not only gives a feeling of strength and support, but one of peace and safety in the classroom.

2. Hanging crystal balls to catch the sunlight will enhance and vitalize the classroom with dancing rainbow colours on sunny days. These days, as well as the rainy ones, can be recorded by the children in a beautiful chart or weather book.

3. Unlock the doors of the classroom, as this facilitates communication between teacher and students. A blocked door can also be harmful to the physical being of the teacher and to her

career. The doors represent the voice of the teacher. Activate the doors if you need more authority.

4. If there is a door that the children are not allowed to use, place a round mirror on the door at their eye level. This allows them to feel included in a world that already belongs to them.

5. In order to create good luck, always have fresh flowers in the room. Use spring flowers in the spring, fall flowers in the fall, and winter flowers in the winter.

6. Nine round pieces of orange peel in one's pocket can lift the teacher's spirit on a difficult day.

7. A crystal ball in the centre of the room will quiet the room.

8. If the teacher's energy is low, put nine fresh green plants in the room.

9. When entering a Kindergarten or nursery room, one's eye feasts on a centre of beauty. This is the first thing one sees on entering. The rest of the room radiates this essential beauty of placement, colour, space. This look into a child's world sets the tone of relationship between the teacher, the environment, and the child.

10. To begin each week, sprinkle bird seed out of the main Kindergarten door to bring a good week and welcome visitors and parents.

11. A bamboo flute hung with its mouthpiece down can bring peace, stability, and good news to a Kindergarten room. When it is played it strengthens weak chi and generally boosts morale.

12. Placing plants in the room symbolizes life and growth. If the plant thrives, so will the children and the teacher. Placed on either side of the entrance they will create and attract good chi. There should be no artificial flowers in the Kindergarten.

A Harmonious Environment

1. In addition to Feng Shui, we teachers know the importance of harmonizing people and places. Each classroom finds both teacher and student feeling the pulse of their surroundings. In her 1993 book The Power of Place, Winnifred Gallagher incorporates many insights from researchers on the link between our internal states

and external environments. Froebel said that you can't change the child, but you can change the environment. Below, I set out some ways in which this can be effected – all of which are tried and tested from my own Kindergarten work. The ambience I strive for is one of peace, and the feeling that one is in the right place at the right time.

The teacher brings into the classroom objects that, for her, evoke memories of her own days as a child, her family, her interests. These cherished gifts give the classroom historic depth that helps the continuity of wholeness.

2. The children should be given the gift of furniture made of wood. The life forces of the tree give the children the opportunity to be grateful to Mother Earth. This caring for a gift from the earth not only builds respect for the furniture but also builds a foundation for the experience that we are one with the earth.

3. All synthetic and plastic material should be removed from the Kindergarten.

4. If the calendar in the room does not include the seasonal mood, as represented by the phase of the moon, the children's and teacher's birthdays, and holidays, the life force of the moment is gone. Since the calendar is written in the sky, the phase of the moon is portrayed in great splendor, the stars hang from the ceiling, and Father Sun is honored.

5. The Kindergarten door opens into a garden. This garden is not only the setting for play, but the entire basis for all art and learning. I count every day as lost when children are not in the garden.

6. Care is taken to establish a feeling of family and togetherness. This can be achieved by having a 'golden ring' in the center of the room where the children form a circle with the teacher. This is not drawn on the floor. All furniture is placed to help establish a feeling of roundness – a completeness balancing out sharp lines.

7. The hanging and placing of coats and lunch-boxes should be an aesthetic experience. No coat should ever be found crying on the floor.

8. Blackboards, if used at all, should be draped, or should bear a colorful anticipation by unveiling a lovely piece of silk that covers over the beautiful drawing that illustrates the story of the week or the celebration of the moment. Exposure to raw chalkboards tends to weaken the child.

9. All containers for crayons, scissors, paper, and so on need to be well-chosen baskets or wooden boxes. What the hand holds is absorbed into the nervous system.

10. Nothing is more demeaning to the 'iris' of the eye than to have the colours of the rainbow presented without imagination and beauty. Iris was the goddess of the rainbow, and each teacher must become like the goddess Iris, in her own creative way presenting the colours of the rainbow in beautiful material adorning the Kindergarten room. This order of the colours brings stability to the life of the five-year-old. The lawfulness and order of the universe are essential to the healthy development of the child.

11. The teacher always sits in a high-back chair such as the mother's lap in order to deal with difficult people or circumstances.

12. Fill the room with song and fragrance before the children arrive.

13. Open up space. We are creating space for the child's and the teacher's creative work to begin and continue. Our job is to bring balance into each life.

14. Every class has seasonal dress-ups available for the children. These are not costumes, but materials that the children can choose to make into whatever their imagination hungers for.

15. Create centres around the room that help the child with his own organization of thought. Here at the Mother Goose centre we say our rhymes of Mother Goose and keep the materials that enrich this important activity.

16. Encourage the children to see a golden chain of life running through every form of existence. We are all connected to the pulse of life. 'All things are all things.'

17. Pentatonic chimes are used as an aid to bring balance in the Kindergarten. The Kindergarten child lives in the realm or mood of the pentatonic.

18. One is always on the lookout for a bell that sounds the 'A' tone for the Kindergarten. This universal sound of 'A' is life-giving to inward harmony. The orchestra strikes 'A' to begin each concert. 'A' is the sound of the universe.

19. If charts are used, they need to be the work of the child or a creative adult artist, not bought from a shop. Uncover in anticipation that which has been covered with beautiful yardage.

20. The forms that the sounds of our English language have taken

should be shown in the sequence of the alphabet in large golden letters placed among the stars on the wall that can be brought down for the child to feel. All the letters that hold the sounds which are gifts from the stars are needed in order for us to write and read our history and give birth to ideas that bind us together. One of these golden upper-case letters first used by the Romans can be brought down and celebrated each week.

21. Likewise, the Indo/Arabic numbers should be given a special, meaningful place in the room. The child needs to feel the power and placement of the numbers within herself. Her numbered place in the 'golden ring' takes on meaning when she can claim it for her own.

The Kindergarten Hand-washing Ritual

Because I feel it is important to wash our hands before eating, I make a ceremony of washing, a ritual I learnt in England. We try to use warm water if possible because dirt can dissolve better at higher temperatures. We use liquid soap so that bacteria will not grow in bars of soap. We wash one hand with the other in a large, stainless steel bowl while we say the 'Silver Sea' poem. I call one child up at a time and say the poem with him. It is calming to both teacher and child before lunch. As I dry their hands I sing the song, 'Dry Hands, Dry', and use a towel that is just the right colour for the season.

On the day the janitor was to put in the paper holder that we were to use to dry our hands, I said no, I could not bear to have the children use all that paper from the trees: it seemed like a perfect waste. So we made small towels, which hang above the sinks. They give us real work to do, in keeping them clean, and they add colour to the room. Each day has its own colour.

PART IV

Celebration

Kindergarten Baby

No Kindergarten has the right to call itself a Kindergarten without the excitement that surrounds the birth of a baby. When I first began teaching, I would hear the chant 'Kindergarten Baby', as older students would spy a Kindergarten child. I have not heard it for years, and I think it is due to the fact that I go above and beyond what is expected to establish the image of the Kindergarten baby. I expect some family each year to give this special and vital gift of a baby to the Kindergarten. It simply would not be a Kindergarten without the birth of a baby for us to celebrate.

Parents have always been generous in providing this vital part of the 'curriculum'. However, there was a year when the birth of a child was not evident. 'We need a Kindergarten baby', I said. I told the parents of the importance of this happening in our Kindergarten. Learning to give is what this year is all about. What better way to perfect the art of gift-giving than to make things in preparation for the arrival of the baby and for the many visits to our classroom. In this way, we get a chance to look at our birth once again from our five-year-old platform.

The child can see the way it was loved, looked after, and enjoyed. 'This is how tiny I was. This is how all of us began. What can I do, make, and give to celebrate this event?' The importance of caring needs to take root now in a group situation. We are all focused on the waiting and on the counting of the time for the arrival of this child whom we have claimed as our own. The big brother or sister of the coming baby ends up feeling like the most important member of the class; they become the centre of attention.

All the Kindergarten babies I have had in my Kindergarten days have grown up to be the best of all students, the most loveable, the kind of people we all want to be. You can recognize them as having something special in their lives. Jonathan, Brad, Alicia, Evan, Matthew, Morgan....

A month later, after I had given this speech to the parents, Kathryn's mother came to me and said, 'We are going to have the Kindergarten baby'. All year long we rejoiced over the coming event. Each of us embroidered a special letter in the alphabet for a quilt that Mert, our wonderful aide, put together for us to give to the baby. In the last week of school, the baby was born, thankfully just in time. The big sister took the invitation home, saying when to arrive in our class for our special party welcoming this Kindergarten baby. It was a day to honour Kathryn, the big sister, just as much as the new baby, in that her status in her new role made her feel more than important. From then on we always referred to Kathryn as the 'Big Sister'.

One year I discovered that the neighbour across the street was pregnant. This freed the other parents from having to volunteer! I asked the neighbour to come and visit the Kindergarten before the baby's birth. When she came, I told the story of how hard it was to find the right place for the baby's beginning days:

'Where would be the very best place in all the world for a new baby to begin its life?' 'Well, we want the baby to begin its life in our nest', said the birds.

'No', said all those who had gathered to search for the right place. 'Why, the wind might blow the nest down and the baby would topple to the ground.'

'We want the baby here', said the rabbits. 'We have a lovely place under the ground near the old fir tree.'

'Oh, no, that would never do. There would be too much company', said the others. 'The baby must have a place that is warm and cozy, plenty of food, a little hot tub, and music. Your place would never do.'

So they searched for a long time. Finally they found just the right place: near to the mother's heart. Here there was music, there was a little hot tub, there was plenty of food, and there was a place that would be warm and cozy.

bp

Do you see how the mother is very much like the letter 'b'? We say, 'First, the mother', as we trace the line down on the 'b'. Then as we trace the round part of the 'b', we say, 'This is how the baby grows'. The children draw it in the air, then on paper they draw the picture of the mother looking very much like a 'b'.

We had made a pillowcase for this occasion, and now we brought pieces of wool to stuff the pillow for the baby. As we presented our gifts of wool to the mother, we told the mother a special wish we had for the baby. 'I wish the baby will be a beautiful princess', said one friend. All the wishes were written down for the family to read over and over again. Soon the little pillow was full of our best wishes, and soft and plump to take home.

Another neighbour who also lived close by our Kindergarten had the Kindergarten Baby for us. The mother was Mary in our Nativity scene two months later, with her new baby for us all to see. Her three-year-old Big Sister was standing by, dressed as the Christmas Angel.

I remember when I was the Big Sister with my Kindergarten Baby. I knew that when my Kindergarten class came to see my new baby, no one needed to call me the big sister. I knew this was my baby, my father, my mother, my house, my Kindergarten, my teacher… the world was mine. How I wish every child could have this experience. I still feel to this day the glow that engulfed me. Yes, it was my baby, but for a brief moment, every child in that Kindergarten claimed that baby as their own. So perhaps you understand why it is that I feel so strongly about including the birth of a baby as a vital part of the Kindergarten curriculum.

I strongly feel that no religion has the right to the story of the birth of a baby. Each year I celebrate the Nativity in my Kindergarten because I know that when a mother gives birth, the angels sing, gifts are brought, and every one gathers around. This wonderful myth of the Christmas Baby is a story of pure poetry… every child's birth… every mother's hope. We hope our newborn has come to save the world. IT IS ONE MORE CHANCE FOR PEACE TO COME TO THE EARTH. It's a story about all of us. A story of fathers taking care of mothers. A story of Innkeepers finding room for others. A story of people leaving what they were doing and going in search of something they believe to be life-giving. A story about the moment of magic that comes when a baby is born and star shine is seen in everyone's eyes.

I remember Adam's mother saying, 'If anyone says you can't give the nativity play, I and my friends will picket outside the classroom door. We will carry signs that say 'JEWISH MOTHERS FOR THE NATIVITY'.

All nine months of waiting for the celebration of birth should be spent planting the garden for the new child... a garden full of herbs, flowers, trees and water lilies, wild grasses... each with its own story forming in your heart to give at just the right time to this new earth child. The stories gathered from mythology, stories of the great gardeners who loved the plants and gave them a touch of themselves, stories of the naming of plants and their origin – all these the parents learn in order to bring the totality of the garden to the child. Then, all the garden talks with the child as though they were a part of each other.

They talk first in repetition, saying the words over and over again, and then slowly grow into the folk tales themselves. Then comes the thinking it all over in terms of rhythm, movement, and music as one first hears and sees it in the garden.

Because the garden is the basis of all art, one marvels with the child about the design, colour, and scent of such an earth as ours. One stands in awe and gratitude at being the beholder of such a gift. Knowing that you can direct and work with these life forces celebrating the diversity of all life gives you a feeling of importance of working hand in hand with nature.

But most of all, the child must feel your gratefulness, for upon this does he build his life. Being thankful is the first step; without this, there is no love. To be truly grateful to the sun, the winds, the clouds, the bees that party with the blossoms, the creatures of the garden, and the herbs that scent the air. This child must be filled with gratitude for all forms that life has chosen; then will come the awe and love of all humankind.

Then comes the careful walking on the rooftop of the gopher snake, then comes the thankfulness to the vegetables and raindrops and the taking care of all the forms that life has chosen.

The child learns to be a lover of ants, of birds and all their secrets. She feels and sees the life into death and death into life and knows that the law of nature is that all things are all things.

And as she learns to play in the garden with sand, rock, and water, she comes to rule herself and discover the gift that she brings to the world.

And when she prepares and eats the food that will nourish her the rest of her life, she will know it as a friend. Having helped bring the plant to birth, then felt her responsibility for its growth, she stretches her world to the beginning of time and becomes one with it.

With this experience, the child then stands on the earth in quite a different way, as though walking on the back of a whale. Alive with the rhythm of the seasons, alive with the stories that now structure her imagination, and fantasies that make her feel that this is truly her earth that has waited all these years for her to arrive.

The Celebration of Christmas

When we come back from Thanksgiving vacation, we already are experiencing the glow of anticipation. The room is now set up with the Christmas colours – red and green. We look on the red December birthday board and observe the four gates to Christmas Day. These we see are the four weeks before Christmas. Each week will have a red candle to help us to welcome our entrance through each gate. These four weeks take us to the birth of the Christmas Baby. One candle is lit each week until all four burn at once to celebrate the day. The number four comes from the earth itself. Four seasons, four directions, four winds, four corners of the earth, the four elements of fire, water, air, and earth. Four is the powerful number that roots us to the earth. Every time we can, we celebrate this number.

The sacredness of numbers is raised to a higher level during this season. At this time in the life for the Kindergarten child, one should make all numbers alive, real, and meaningful. One can do this through the counting down of the 25 days until Christmas. This counting process can be practised to enhance your heritage or background in every way. On birthdays one can ring out the bell tones that count each year you have lived. This celebration is vital to the family.

One can count 25 angels coming down, or 25 trees or shrubs planted and lit one night at a time. A collection of brass candle-holders, and each holding a beeswax candle waiting its turn to be lit. Stars marked in gradual sizes till you reach 25, which is the largest of all. Twenty-five story books to read and re-read each year or each night during Advent.

And of course I use an Advent calendar, which shows the 25 days that take us to Christmas. There are many kinds of Advent calendars; the one I have was made by John's father, cut from wood and standing on the floor. Each day is represented by a different shape window that is placed in a spiral form, so that the last window is in the centre. We open it to find a picture of the baby.

The windows we open show the picture of the songs and poems we know. Two elves – which suggests the song, The Elves and the Shoemaker's true gift. A rainbow overhead; for the rainbow song I wrote:

I LIGHT THIS CANDLE

Betty Peck

I light this can-dle, then I say, thank you for the love-ly day.

Thank you for this candlelight, that turns our darkness into light. Who made this candle, I'd

like to know, that sends its love-ly, gold-en glow, so that we can see all the

col- ors we know that live up in the rain - bow.

Then other pictures of our poems, songs, and stories appear in the nativity windows:

- ♦ pictures of a donkey, cow, sheep, and dove – for the French carol, 'The Friendly Beasts';
- ♦ red roses – for the song, 'The Christmas Garden';
- ♦ a star – for 'Twinkle, Twinkle, Little Star';
- ♦ a yellow sun – for 'The Sun Shines Bright Above';

- ◆ a Christmas Tree – for 'O Tannenbaum';
- ◆ blue mother – for 'The Mary Song';
- ◆ a crescent moon – for 'The Moon is Growing in Full Face';
- ◆ purple kings – for the song about the letter K, 'I am the King,' and 'We Three Kings;
- ◆ holly – for 'The Holly and the Ivy';
- ◆ a shepherd – for 'Shepherd's Maiden';
- ◆ bells – for 'I heard the bells on Christmas Day';
- ◆ Mary – for 'Child and Mother';
- ◆ Jacob Macabee – for Hanukkah songs;
- ◆ an angel – for 'Angels We Have Heard on High';
- ◆ a Christmas sock – for the story of the 'Dutch child;'
- ◆ a wreath – for the song, 'Christmas Will Come Again';
- ◆ a sleigh – for 'Jingle Bells';
- ◆ gifts – for the poem 'Open the Gate of my Heart and Give';
- ◆ birthday cake on the 18th for my Birthday Celebration song;
- ◆ manger scene for the song 'Away in a Manger'.

This sequence of our songs and stories gives us a feeling of direction and accomplishment. In Kindergarten everything must be a part of everything else, so that we draw the world around us and feel welcomed and sure of the path we take. How do we gather the stillness of the centre of all the hurried activities of these days and make it ours so that the mood of this season can enrich us and those around us forever? I find that the art of gift-making becomes all-inclusive.

'What are you giving for Christmas?' is the question in the Kindergarten. The letter that holds the sound of 'G' with its gestures is chosen for this week: 'I open the gates of my heart and give, and when I do, it makes it possible for everything to come back to me.' What is this giving?

True Gift

As I visited in the home of Dean's mother, she showed with pride the artwork of her friend, Pat, that now decorated her house. Pat was there and her feeling of pleasure and pride could be felt by all of us. Then when I went to Pat's house and Dean's mother's artwork was hanging on Pat's walls, it was Dean's mother who now shone with joy and pleasure at the showing of each piece she had made for her friend, Pat.

I came back the next day to the Kindergarten and wrote this poem:

There are many gifts.
But a true gift is something you make,
Because you make it with your imagination,
Your time, your money,
Your hands,
Your brain, and your best wishes.
You are really wrapping yourself up
And giving yourself away.
Of course, that means there is more of you everywhere.
And when you bump into pieces of your good old wonderful self,
Sparkles fill the air.

Poetry from the Kindergarten floor.

bp

I invite the parents for an evening on this vital subject of gift-giving, long before the season begins. I have always talked of Emerson's writing on this subject. At this time of year, when darkness is all about, we seek the light. We are longing for its return. Some of the ways we celebrate are by making candles, by planting bulbs that bury the light, by making tissue-paper windows, by having Advent calendars with light showing through the windows, and by using rainbows for bending the light, made out of the colours of the rainbow for each child. Out of each bag the dancing teacher (the prism) comes to bend the light for us, so that the light-dancers dance around the room in seven-coloured dancing gowns. The cloth bags are the little houses in which the prisms live.

At school their pictures are full of rainbows – it is a sign that you have arrived on earth when the rainbows flood your pictures. We work in a room filled with rainbows. All the colours that we use are kept in our rainbow area. Pens, water colours, honey crayons, and inks are kept beneath draped, hand-dyed, rainbow-coloured gauze. Our capes are hung in rainbow order; our towels are hung in rainbow order; our crayons are kept in rainbow order; our cubbies are in rainbow order in the Rainbow Room. The importance of this orderly following of the colours gives an enormous sense of belonging to the cosmos. To be able to say the rainbow colours by heart is a thrilling moment for the child. The words 'by heart' are by no means overlooked.

How do you decorate the house at Christmas? What can you gather of family artifacts around you? What can you gather from the earth that shows your caring of this great hovering spirit, nourisher of our body and soul, that we lovingly call Mother Earth? What symbols of other cultures that you include and now call your own, because they have touched your heart and resonated in the depths of your soul, that you can bring to fill your house?

The celebration of Christmas comes in many forms in our Kindergarten. Having children in the class with Dutch backgrounds, one cannot overlook the great day of Saint Nicholas. From all the stories of Saint Nicholas, I use the one about Saint Nicholas on his white horse, arriving at the window of the poor merchant who had no dowry for his three daughters. He threw a bag of gold into the open window. This happened again for the second daughter. When the third daughter needed a dowry, the father himself waited in the shadows to see who it was who had been so kind to his first two daughters. He could see someone as he came close to the window to throw the bag of gold for the dowry of the third daughter. He called to him, 'Who are you?' 'Please', he said, 'I am Nicholas, but do not tell anyone about my deeds until after my death'.

As a child, Saint Nicholas lived in a monastery and became used to a simple way of life. He inherited a lot of money later, and gave it all to the poor. Throughout his life he gave gold and food to the hungry without anyone knowing who it was who had given them these gifts. Because of all his golden deeds, he was called Saint Nicholas.

Traditionally Saint Nicholas comes with Black Peter, Ruprick, who is his comical companion. Black Peter brings his switches and he accompanies Saint Nicholas as he travels on his birthday, 6th December. Saint Nicholas' golden book is kept in our Kindergarten with all the brothers' and sisters' names written in from previous classes. Golden deeds are recorded in this book.

What books do you now unveil and bring from their tucked-away areas for the celebration of this night of nights? What songs pour forth from your heart that long have been a part of the universal lifting-up of ourselves and others through the ages into being greater and more than what we are and ever could be without them? What sounds and sights and smells propel us into the heights of sensuous richness of the season? What recipes do we again gather from old family days, that now take on a new meaning?

At times the Kindergarten class has been away when Saint Nicholas arrives. It is then that we take off our shoes and place them in the Golden Ring, as we are called into the library to hear a story. When we return, we find tangerines, golden walnuts, and cookies in our shoes. But some have been known to find just switches. To acknowledge wrong is an important positive action. As teachers, we deal with this in many ways. Finding the switches clears the air for all of us. The others know of the misdeeds of their friends and they also know that they themselves will be dealt with fairly when their time comes. As teachers we demand the best from everyone's wonderful self.

At this moment of discovery of the sticks, all is hushed. The hand of justice is powerful in the silence. Then Black Peter throws the golden nuggets (cookies) into the room, and all the children scramble for them. A black-gloved hand rises over the rainbow partition in the back of the room, over and over, again and again, throwing the golden nuggets. If the children find gold threads along the path where Saint Nicholas has been, they know it is more real than real. And so we find the golden threads along the path to our garden gate, where he has mounted his white horse and disappeared. Saint Nicholas has left two capes, woven with golden deeds, that will be worn each day by a different boy and girl who everyone knows has done a golden deed. The cape stays in our room for the rest of the year. The boys' cape is solid gold. The girls' cape is dotted with gold.

In the last few years Saint Nicholas himself has come to our classroom. We have found him waiting silently for us on our return back to the room. He stands tall and straight as we enter, wearing his bishop's hat and long robes. The children are awed by his presence. He holds in his hand 'The Book of Golden Deeds'. He calls each child up and puts his hand on their head as he reads from The Book of Golden Deeds. The golden deeds of each child are read aloud. Their heads shake to affirm his record. 'Yes', says Jeff, 'I do take good care of the bricks'.

He then gives them each a tangerine and a golden walnut. He talks about the importance of golden deeds. After he leaves, we also find golden-deed capes that he has left for us. And yes, someone discovers along the path, gold leading to our garden gate. We now know he was truly in our Kindergarten.

Now begins the choosing of the activities that must fill these days with the richness of spirit, the beauty of activity, and the joy of anticipation. There are many to choose from. How does one choose? It is the teacher's philosophy that shines forth. It is here that experience takes the lead. What memories does she bring to this moment? How was it handled in her family when she was this age? What impression did she gain? What has been her journey into the meaning of celebration? How has the celebration with her own family grown through the gatherings of her own journey? What is her life's meaning? What resonates within her as the year draws to an end? As she now enters into these days that bring both the high point and holy night of the year, how does she handle it, both with parents and children?

I bring to the parents, first, the importance of the mood of anticipation; second, the importance of the true gift; and third, the universal importance of the birth of the child, our love, our Messiah, ourselves. The mood is set by the growing darkness, and we find ourselves becoming quieter, with curtains being pulled to create this feeling of cozy winter days. We sing 'Now Cometh Gentle Mother Night,' to feel the mother's arms enfolding us.

The story-form holds the essence of the season. The first story of the holidays is 'The Elves and the Shoemaker'. Never was there such a story that spelled out true gift-giving. When the children present this story on Friday as a play, we have a chorus of the striking clock. This is the time to bring in the most beautiful clock, with finger numbers (Roman numerals) and a beautiful chime. The symbol of the clock becomes a farewell gesture to the old year.

Our stories always end with singing rhythmic activity to come out of the mood of the story. The song 'The Shoemaker's Wife' is one of the children's and parents' favourites, for, all of a sudden, gift-giving becomes real. Gift-giving is what you and I do for each other. It is what we make, what we sing, what we use to surprise, what we help with. Gift-giving is freed of money and vacant gestures of things, want, and greed. Our letter for the week is 'G':

> 'When I open the gate of my heart and give.
> Then everything comes back to me.'
>
> bp

Then we plunge into making gifts and wrapping paper. Wrapping things up is the gesture of wrapping yourself up and giving your very own self away. It is the symbol of your outer selves that houses your own golden heart. To wrap or enclose with ourselves and our love cuddled around a package waiting for the moment of revealing the truth. The kernel of joy, the beauty of myself to you... the surprise... the anticipation... the birth... the dark womb to the light of day... the 'giving poem'... the light. It is the rich symbolism of Christmas and there are twelve days of it.

How important to have the Italian tale of Old Befana sweeping and cleaning her house. But more must take place before we enter into the Legend of the Kings. The story of the fir tree is told, about how he comes as an arrow to the earth from the bow of Cupid. It is a beautiful story of why we have the Christmas tree – no child should be without it. In the story, the arrow becomes the fir tree, and after it has fallen to the earth, it longs to be back among the stars. Even so, his heart melts for the barren earth. The creatures ask him to call down the stars – he finds he can call them down. The stars become the flowers scattered over the earth. And because of this deed, once each year the tree is decorated with sparkling stars and children dance around it.

THE FIR TREE

Betty Peck

The ar-row fell to the bar-ren earth,and gave to the evergreen tree its birth, and the

stars they twin-kled all a-round, all a-round, and the stars they twin-kled all a- round.

The arrow fell to the barren earth,
And gave to the evergreen tree its birth.
> CHORUS:
> And the stars they twinkled all around, all around
> And the stars they twinkled all around,

The fir tree lowered, its branches down,
Until they reached the dear old ground.
> CHORUS

The roots reached out and hugged the stars,
The rocks and the stones and the dinosaur bones.
> CHORUS

Tell us the story of the stars,
So that they can also be ours.
> CHORUS

bp

We learn to cut the evergreen tree from folded paper in all sizes and shapes. These are used in a myriad of ways: around our room, for decorations, and on cards. We print with them. The form of the evergreen tree strengthens our structural pattern of the triangle.

Our letter is now 'S' for star. (The first letter for this season was 'G', for giving and gifts.) When we lie down on yellow paper and are traced around, head, two outstretched arms, and two outstretched legs, we discover that we, too, are stars. Heather once said, 'I think I was born a star'. And so we all are five-pointed stars.

After each child has cut out his huge yellow star, which is a picture of herself, I move these from one place to another in the room; and after we have had our star parade through the halls of the school, we return one morning to find them all on the ceiling, singing their star songs in a golden ring above our heads. Now we know that we are the most wonderful Kindergarten under the stars. On occasion they fall down, and we find another place for these fallen stars in our room, or we take them home. I tell the children that they will learn when they are older that we are all made of stardust.

We have a quilt in the shape of a star. A child can lie on it by finding the 'T', for top, which shows him where to place his head. He lies down, matching his shape with this yellow star with its five points in the middle of the golden ring. After he lies down, we think of everything that is proud to be five and we sing a special song:

A STAR INSIDE THE APPLE

Betty Peck and Anna Rainville

There is a star inside the apple, 1, 2, 3, 4, 5.
    CHORUS:
    Oh, I can shine and I can smile
    And I can sparkle like you.

My right hand has five fingers, I, 2, 3, 4, 5.
  CHORUS
My left hand has five fingers, 1, 2, 3, 4, 5.
  CHORUS
The starfish has five arms, 1, 2, 3, 4, 5.
  CHORUS
Shiro has five years, 1, 2, 3, 4, 5.
  CHORUS
  [This verse is sung with everyone's name who has five years.]
The wild rose has five petals, 1, 2, 3, 4, 5.
  CHORUS

bp

Saint Valentine's Day

Saint Valentine's Day comes next in our celebration of life in the Kindergarten. Bird song is everywhere, and we soon realize the reason for the bird song, for Saint Valentine's day is the day the birds find their sweethearts and begin their nest-building. The Kindergarten children take out wool, ribbon, and yarn, and tuck them on trees, fences, shrubs, and all likely places where they can be found by the birds to help with their nest-building.

During this season the winter wind usually brings a nest to us. What materials did the birds use to build this nest? We see many things in the nest that the birds have used from our garden. We stretch out a long piece of paper across the room on which we place and admire each little twig and piece of grass, horsehair, and so on. We take the nest apart one piece at a time. We count each twig as we undo the nest. We draw a little nest around each ten pieces to make our counting easier. It is amazing how many trips these birds made in order to collect all that they have brought to this nest.

After many days of admiring the weaving skills of the birds and their genius, I say, 'Let's put it all back together again'. 'Impossible…' – but we try. With this experience we will always look with great admiration at those tiny creatures of the air that know many things we shall never know.

The month called February, the second month of the year, plunges us into two-ness. We do everything in twos. A heart sitting on a firm foundation is made by drawing two number twos facing each other. We must truly love ourselves first, but the expansion and reaching out to another is the beginning of true love. Did you ever wonder why Saint Valentine's birthday is celebrated in the second month of the year?

Saint Valentine himself has left us with many myths that we try to piece together. In my Kindergarten I tell the story like this:

Long ago there was a man named Valentine who loved to write letters filled with love. Valentine gathered oak balls from the oak trees that grew in Rome. He discovered how to make ink from them. When he couldn't find them, he used the black soot from his lamp. This, mixed with egg white from his chickens and water from his rain barrel, gave him the ink that was needed in order to draw with his quill pen. These beautiful feathers that he used as pens are from the wings of the bird. Do you know why it is that the wing feathers are used?

> 'Lovely golden letters are in my heart.
> Lovely golden letters are in my heart.
> They sit beside each other so that they can fly
> Just like a bird from me to you.'

And so from Valentine's heart to the paper would fly his words of love.

When Valentine was thrown into prison because he was a Christian, the jailer knew he was a man of letters. The jailer had a daughter who was blind. He asked Valentine if he could tutor his daughter. She was quick to learn, and she soon regained her eyesight. She had learned to write and read. When Valentine was put to death, a letter was found in his prison cell. The letter was for his pupil, the jailer's daughter. It was signed, 'From your Valentine'.

GOLDEN LETTERS

Betty Peck

Love-ly gol-den let-ters are in my heart.

Love-ly gol-den let-ters are in my heart. They sit be- side each

oth-er so that they can fly just like a bird from me to you.

This is the story of the first Valentine. However, I've heard it told that the birds came to the prison window and carried off the other letters of love that Valentine had written. They were delivered everywhere.

The next year on Valentine's birthday the world again was filled with letters of love. This happened each year. Because of this, he was chosen for sainthood. On his birthday every 14th of February, we celebrate Saint Valentine's Day because of the man who knew how to put his love into words. It is important, I believe, always to remember to say Saint Valentine, for all too soon are we disconnected from our roots.

Saint Valentine's friend, Bruce, comes to our Kindergarten with white turkey wing feathers to make into quills. He is surrounded by the children as he writes our beautiful letters with such majesty and care. The way he handles paper shows his love and care. No wonder he treats the paper so lovingly, for he tells how this beautiful paper he calls parchment is made from his sheep. All the children watch him as he prepares the parchment.

In Kindergarten, nothing must be taken for granted. All layers must be peeled back to find the freshness of new birth. To be able to talk with someone who loves writing so much, and be able to watch him as he works with his craft, gives children deep appreciation for the art we call writing.

Yes, the making of Valentines links the child with the past, with nature; and because of the richness of the moment, it puts him in touch with the future. When I ask every child to form a nest with his hands, I drop a little red egg into their warm bird's nest. They must keep it warm while I tell the story about this piece of red beeswax:

Not far from here is a little village. In the village are lots of houses. They are not at all like our houses in many ways, but then, they are very much like ours. The babies are born. The babies are fed. The workers bring food. Their houses all have six sides.

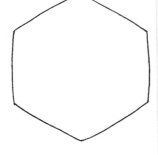

When you draw these houses, you draw the north side and the south side connected by bent arms. When they are all filled with food, the workers leave them and build other houses.

We know the builders, and we eat their food. The builders and workers all have a queen that sings the same song, always on the same note: A-A-A-A-A-A.

What creatures besides us sing the 'A'? Yes, it is the bee, and the story is about the beehive, and the six-sided houses in the beehive are made of beeswax. And when the farmer needs honey, he finds that there is always plenty of honey for himself and the bees. For the bees are the busiest of all creatures and no one ever has to tell them what to do, for they always know their job.

They work all day, having tea parties with the flowers. When they are full of the sweet tea which the flowers give them, they make a bee-line home and soon the little wax house is filled with honey.

After the farmer has taken the honey from the bees he has this beeswax left. 'Oh, please', says his wife, 'May I have the beeswax? I will make candles from the beeswax. When I light them here in the evening the fragrance from the flowers will fill the room.' When she saves beeswax for her children to play with, she finds colours in the garden. 'Please, red berries, may I have some of your red?' She mixes it with the beeswax to make red wax to play with and for red candles. When the candles are lit at story-time, she always remembers to thank the bees that hold this little light from the sun.

After the story, the children tell me their little red eggs are soft. The children discover that they are holding balls of red beeswax. And I say, 'Here we are on Saint Valentine's Day. What can we make with our beautiful balls of red beeswax?' In no time at all we have little red hearts that we use in many different ways for our Saint Valentine's gifts.

Every child makes a beautiful Saint Valentine's Box at home – this little box will be the house for his valentines. They are placed on Saint Valentine's Street. I use the window sill, that stretches across the room for this street. The number used for the children's places in the Golden Ring are their address on Saint Valentine's Street in front of their plates. Their names and house numbers on Saint Valentine's Street are written on a heart hanging on the sill that I call Saint Valentine's Street. Each heart opens to show their photograph. Each child brings his own handmade Valentines to mail to each friend who lives on Saint Valentine's Street. What a time it is finding everyone's Valentine Box! 'I love you' signs are placed not only around the room, but they are placed around the entire school by the children.

Of course, the letter 'V' is the sound of Saint Valentine's Week. There are never enough days to celebrate Saint Valentine's Day. Weeks before, we were cutting out hearts and practising reading each others' names. We have made large hearts carrying our names, and we have read and re-read them before they are placed on Saint Valentine's Street. They were placed on the wall in the Moon-Boat area in the order of their chairs. It is here that they discover that there are many ways to teach yourself to read. They learn to read the names by learning the Moon-Boat order; or they can lift the heart and read the photograph; or they can read the beginning sound of the name or the shape of the name as a whole. Each one discovers her own way to read the names.

Each year I read Raggedy Ann, that heart-warming story from my childhood. It is in this story of love and caring hearts that say 'I love you' that we set the stage for Saint Valentine's Week. Never has it failed to bring us all closer together.

By the time we have finished the book, it only seems right that we draw Raggedy Ann's picture, the one we have come to know as our friend. I am always delighted to find these pictures hanging framed in the homes of former students. Lael has hers hanging in the family kitchen – I always plead with mothers to frame at least one picture from the Kindergarten days. Rich is the child who is surrounded by moments of pure joy when their pictures bring to memory the days when they were five years old.

When the Saint Valentine party begins, the curved table is filled with edible Valentines – a tray of cupcakes, cookies, and so on… Tim's mother has sent in a beautiful violet 'V' made of two columns of hearts meeting in a point. The hearts are heart-shaped cookies and they are intermingled with green leaves of candied fruit and violets. Words in gold on red paper bring us greetings from this family. It is a work of art!

The room is filled with red, pink, and white, with a bit of lavender and purple here and there. The children have put up hearts everywhere. They have stuffed small felt hearts with lavender from our garden to wear on a long crochet chain around their necks. In the morning when they come through the garden gate, they find hearts hanging from the trees. They add their homemade ones.

Eric's family has brought in hyacinths in pinks, whites, and reds. Then Katie's family brings in three red tulips each for all the teachers. Three tulips carry the secret message: I love you! The Kindergarten delights in secret, coded messages of every kind.

When the first tulip comes into the room, we gather for the beautiful love story of the tulips. This is the introduction from Nature herself. Because of the story that we read about tulips, the word 'multiply' echoes around the room. It is a word of meaning to them now. The gnome named Times has taught them their first step into the life of multiplication.

As their ticket to the party, the children must find a heart-shaped leaf in the garden to place in the middle of the Golden Ring. Then when they are all seated in the Golden Ring, the Queen of Hearts is chosen first. The King of Hearts is chosen next; then the Prince of Hearts and the Princess of Hearts. They sit on their golden thrones and announce that the party will begin. The bells ring 'A'. (Materials to throw over structures to form thrones are always plentiful. One never knows when the royal thrones will be needed.)

The Saint Valentine's party begins! I pass out my Valentines first. They are three small heart cookies, beautifully wrapped together in red and white. They carry the secret of Saint Valentine's message, and all of the children try to guess what it is. I want them to know the importance of symbolism and what lies beyond, that never is anything without meaning, and that things can be more than they are.

Then someone is chosen to pass out Nancy's Valentines, from our garden friend. Now the tone of festivity is set. Nancy Payne, lover of gardens, makes Valentines of heart stickers, gold, and silver doilies, 'I love you', feathers, glitter, and so on. They can be looked at for ever. Then comes all the eating of Valentines that do not fit in the Saint Valentine Boxes. There we sit, all of us, opening up our Saint Valentine Boxes, trying to call out thank-yous to everyone. We are caught up in the noisy sounds of pure delight. Jamie has given all of us bird whistles and slowly, one after another, the room fills with bird songs.

As I see by the clock that our Kindergarten is closing, I sing the names of two birds to fly together to me for goodbye hugs:

TWO LITTLE BIRDS

Betty Peck

Two lit-tle birds fly a- way.   Jake and Ad-am now fly a- way.

Fly a- way, oh, fly a- way.   Fly a- way, oh, fly a- way.

Spring

There are never enough days to celebrate Spring. Spring days are the days we have been waiting for. New life is everywhere. The birthday board of Spring green sets the colour scheme for the Kindergarten room. Spring green is everywhere in the Kindergarten. I always wore dresses of Spring green. The dress-ups now have lots of Spring green material for the children to use in as many ways as they can think of. Spring flowers of white, yellow, and pastel colours fill the room. Pussy willows are brought in for us all to see and feel and welcome them with our poems and songs about pussy willows.

There were always blossoms brought into the room and we could watch Spring green leaves appear on the long blossom stems. It was my daughter who thought of the idea of having one family each week be responsible for the flowers of the week.

One of the first things to be done is Spring cleaning, which takes place even before the Spring flowers arrive. When the children first enter Kindergarten they are given a special place in the room to call their own. This is where the Sandman will always find them in their cleaned nest. The children clean and polish their nest first. Then there is everything else in the room that must shine – chairs, tables, cupboards, instruments, tools, sinks, and so on. Mothers take the dress-ups home to wash after a Winter of play. Spring cleaning lasts for several days.

I always felt it was important to be outdoors gathering Spring through all of our senses to carry with us for ever. One important area was the nearby orchards that were in full bloom. These field trips found us dancing around the trees and playing games, delighting in the fragrance and beauty of Spring. Our city had preserved a prune and apricot orchard, and this Heritage Orchard, as it is now called, welcomed us each Spring, tended by Matthew and George, who with their mother while they were in my Kindergarten class, would always welcome us to their cherry orchard. I think if I did not have orchards nearby, I would dress each child like a blossoming tree and pretend that Spring had come to our schoolroom orchard.

Lady Spring would come each year to my Kindergarten. She would arrive after Spring cleaning when the room was aglow with Spring itself. She was always dressed in Spring green, carrying a basket of green apples for our Kindergarten days ahead. We sang the Lady Spring Song that started with the words: 'My Lady Spring is dressed in green', and so on.

Spring brings again the magic of seeds. We spend a great deal of time immersing ourselves in the awe and mystery of the 'seed'. How could something this small hold so much? How could all the patterns, colour, texture, and fragrance be hidden inside the seed? And the fact that the seed and its growth needs us to fulfil its life, places the responsibility on us to help make the earth beautiful.

We plant wheat seeds in our baskets that we will use for Easter, and in a planter box made especially for our indoor garden. Once, when the grass was about four inches high, I came into the room one morning and found it had all fallen over, pointing toward our eastern windows. When the children arrived, I said, 'Why do you think the grass has fallen over toward the East? 'Easter is coming', was their immediate reply.

So after that year when it didn't fall over, I pushed it over.

Easter

Now 'Easter is coming' involves being caught up in the cosmos. Easter connects us to the universe, the moon, the Spring Solstice, the sun, and the days of the week. No child should be robbed of knowing this important connection. Easter is not a fixed date.

> Easter comes on the first Sunday
> After the full moon
> After the Spring Solstice.

Therefore the date of the Easter celebration changes every year. It is important that every Kindergarten have the North Star placed on the ceiling of its room. It was early man who felt the awe and wonder of the black night-sky filled with stars that became the textbook of daily life. Small children feel this connection to the moon and its phases. As we know, the calendar is written in the sky. But also the directions of North, South, East, and West – how to bring these directions down on to clay, parchment, and then paper was the task of our early ancestors.

Because the top of the paper was symbolic of the placement of the heavens above, this spot was chosen for North. When we look north, we find that the East is on the right-hand side. And so it is true of our direction East on our maps. But it is also true of our letter 'E'. The capital letters are always presented first in the Kindergarten... no different from the historic beginnings of our alphabet....

The letters are gifts from the stars, so above the gold letters of the alphabet placed in the Kindergarten room are stars. This helps to show the direction of coming down to the earth line below. Then with the letter 'E', it shows the direction of East. Then with the lower-case 'e', we start at the top along the path to the East and say, 'When we walk toward the East, we find that the world is not flat but round.'

Every Kindergarten teacher knows the joy children have in discovering. One of the most wonderful Easter discoveries is the finding of 'earth eggs' in the garden. One Easter morning, my brother, who was newly divorced, appeared at my door with his three children. At that time I had given up the Easter I had been connected with: Up From the Grave He Arose. There was nothing in my house that spoke of Easter. I looked at those three darlings and knew I had to do something. All I had in the house were potatoes that I could use. I cooked them and wrapped them in foil and hid them all over the garden. 'The Easter Rabbit has left "earth eggs" in my garden', I said. What a delightful time they had hunting for them. Since that time I have involved myself in the message of new life that Easter brings. We celebrate with Easter sunrise celebrations, hunts of all kinds, and so on. I find a little bit of death and resurrection every day in my life.

We have hunted for 'earth eggs' ever since. One year in the Kindergarten we had a whole wheelbarrow full of little 'earth eggs' that we have grown in our own garden, which prompted a child to say, 'Mrs Peck, they look a lot like potatoes to me'. 'And so they do', I exclaimed. They are cooked and placed in foil with butter and hidden in the garden by the Easter Hare. Do tell the story of the Easter Hare. My children would delight in making nests for themselves as the hare does from wild flowers and tall grasses. The hare lives on top of the earth alone, not like some of our rabbits that live under the ground in warrens. Hares are born with their eyes open, unlike their rabbit cousins who are born naked with their eyes closed.

In Germany and other European Countries, it was the Easter Hare who brought the Easter eggs. The hare was connected with Easter because it was the hare that would come to rescue an exhausted hare who was being chased. This was done by exchanging places with the tired one and running in his place, so the story goes. This belief became connected with the egg which contained new life. It was looked upon as containing the Easter message. The eggs were decorated in many ways, according to the culture of the country.

There are never enough days to celebrate Spring. We have hunts every day as we wait for the real Easter to come. Sometimes we make paper eggs that we design in our own way; sometimes it is peanuts; sometimes we wrap egg-shaped cookies we have made. The children put on rabbit ears if they are the ones chosen to hide the eggs. For in life it is the hunt and search and the discovery that compose our life's journey. Spring green is everywhere and we spend our time looking for new life that appears on every level of our earthly existence.

Dears,

The Persian New Year comes in the Spring.... Today we celebrated with Ronak Kordestani and her parents their Persian New Year. This celebration will always be part of my life. It is so wonderful to have the deep roots of culture come to us from such an ancient land through the lives of our Kindergarten children. I myself feel enriched from the celebration and realize how new our country is... how fast we have grown... and how much our own celebration of New Year needs to look at ancient celebrations when life was rich with mystery, awe, and wonder.

On this day Jonathan and Bryan built the table in the middle of the Golden Ring. And when it was well balanced, Casey, Kate, and Amy decorated it with white... white flowers and veils and wisps of netting. There will be six treasures representing all that is important in our lives. Sarti placed the seven candles on the table. 'S' is the path the stars take as they bring their gifts down to the earth for us. All six treasures must start with the letter 'S'. Katie remembered that our room number started with the letter 'S'. Our room number is seven.

Here are the six treasures starting with 'S':

First, the Sun... the sun's golden rays bring new life to our earth.

Second, the Stars... that guard the happenings of the earth.

Third, the Spices from the earth that smell so good... Joanna brought hers from her mother's herb store and saw to it that they were shared.

Fourth were the Seeds... Chris put wheat seeds on the table. The important treasure houses.

Fifth were the Scriptures... the holy and most important words in all of Persia are collected in one book.

Sixth was the mirror... to see our wonderful Selves and be grateful for all that is around us.

Scott, Chris, and Katie made red stars and red moon to put in the growing wheat. This was tied with a red ribbon to remind us of our flowing blood that is given new life with the coming of Spring. Our gold sun was put in the tall wheat grass nearby in our indoor garden… in gratitude for another year filled with warmth and light.

Alexi, Ryan, Murphy, Jessica, and Casey had made the fire with logs… red and yellow colours and now all was ready…. Everyone worked in their own joyous noisy ways… so that when everything was ready, we not only felt the silence but were ready for it.

Ronak's parents sat on each side of her at the table. First, the mother spoke in her beautiful language, then the father. The first treasure they touched was the book of all their wonderful words. They showed their love of these words in a special way that we all understood, and after they said their greetings to each other, they blew out the seven candles. Their language was important for us to hear… words we didn't understand but felt with our hearts.

The next part of the celebration was to jump over the fire, leaving all our bad dreams, sick days, and trouble to be bundled up while we gathered the colours of the fire to take with us into the New Year… the yellow for bright, warm days ahead after Winter's cold days, the red for vitality that runs in our veins. Everyone jumped over the fire seven times to take in all the beauty from the colours of the fire. When the fire was out, all that was left were the ashes of our troubled days. We will take the colour with us into the New Year.

The children were served the dried fruits and nuts of last year's gifts from the earth, so that we could eat them while waiting for the fresh fruits of Summer. Ronak gave us all books and coloured pencils for us to go from step to step and write down all our wonderful words that go from left to right, while the Persian written language of her family goes from right to left.

Symbolic gifts were given to the children, and a piece of handmade jewellery with seven symbolic fish in old silver was given to me. It never ceases to draw admiration when I wear it.

This celebration showed me how much we need others from ancient countries to share themselves with us in order to make the balance that is needed to enrich our lives. And for all the Ronaks everywhere in Iran, how rich you are in all the ways we know so little about. And for all the Ronaks in our own country, how much we need to open our arms to you for our own healing and new life. This is what Kindergarten is all about.

Hugs,
bp

May Day

Maypole dancing has always been a part of my life. When my daughter was old enough to hold the ribbons, we set up a Maypole in the front garden on a small patch of lawn. At that time, the Maypole was a tether ball pole embedded in concrete that was held by a tyre. We covered the foundation with spring-coloured cloths and flowers. The smilax vines growing freely in our garden have become a part of all our celebrations over the years. With garlands of smilax and ribbons hanging from the top of the pole covered with flowers, this became our first Maypole.

Her love of the Maypole embedded itself in my daughter so deeply that she carried it to her days of teaching at her Waldorf School in Lexington, Massachusetts. At that time, old Winter would grumble at the thought of Spring coming, and just at that moment, Lady Spring would drop a bouquet down from the window above and welcome all of her Spring Days. This was the sign for the May Dance to begin.

When the Community Garden was established, the first thing we did was to put in a grass circle to accommodate Maypole dancing. Before this, we would stand in the tall grasses and sing French May Day carols and eat strawberry shortcake with friends early on a May morning. Then we would be off to work.

A beautiful hand-carved Maypole was made by Charles Griffin, our garden manager, for this celebration that we held now at noontime. We gathered for lunch and had May Day dancing afterwards.

My Kindergarten children would come dressed in their best for May Day. All the flowers from the garden were used to decorate the garlands. Big baskets of flowers for the tables and a flower crown for the top of the Maypole were gathered. Imagine having more flowers than one could possibly use. Ruth Rees from the Rees Iris Society gave us the iris that surrounded the circle of grass. One was a light apricot colour: We chose this colour for the May Day Queen's costume and have used it ever since. I can remember the May Day Queen carrying large bouquets of iris, roses, and dripping smilax that Alicia's mother had made.

We decided that strawberry shortcake would be the best of all May Day foods. What a time it was to find the most beautiful strawberries for all those who would attend. We never knew how many would come. But strawberries were always topped by Mr. Peake's cream from his local Claravale Dairy, well known to all the children. We would see him coming down the long country road carrying the container filled with bottles of cream. Then we knew that the celebration could begin.

It was a production to get the cream whipped. My electric beaters are forever lost at the garden. Tablecloths, dishes, paper plates, spoons, vases, and baskets were all piled into my car, along with the round tables for the May Day feast early that May morning.

We were always delighted to see the caller come in costume for the adult dancing. The caller and the strawberries were always my treat to everyone. It was a real celebration of May, and gold cannot buy these kinds of memories when everyone helps make it a special day.

It was a very hard job to round up just the right combination of musicians for the day. I do feel that a celebration must start by rounding up the musicians first – sometimes it would take me several weeks to find them. These charming young people who have found one of the great secrets of life – the joy of music – would gather to play for our dancing.

Of course, the Kindergarten children would lead the procession down to the Maypole from the garden amphitheatre after the crowning of the May Day Queen. Sometimes the goats, all decorated with garlands of flowers, would join us. We would play our tambourines and sing, and each child would then hold her yellow or green ribbon from the Maypole. And the music and dancing would begin. After our dances, the children gave the ribbons to the adults, and the children watched the adults plait the ribbons around the Maypole. Then a great web of ribbons would be formed around the pole, stretching out like a tent during the next Maypole dance.

Our last May Day at the garden was beautiful. All the activities took place in the centre of the garden. The throne for the Queen reached the overhanging black walnut tree's branches. This throne was filled with flowers. Anna, the May Day Queen, was dressed in the beautiful, delicate, apricot gown with a bouquet to match and attendants carrying her train. Everyone cheered, and the Queen welcomed us all to join in this ancient celebration that has brought joy to young as well as old from years past.

When the great ten-acre demonstration garden was to be subdivided, the question, of course, was where May Day should be held. I found just the right place to have a Maypole celebration on the far east corner of the lawn at our school. On Sundays the Recreation Department is in charge of all school activities, so I would have had to work with them. It all seemed too much. So I decided we would hold it where we had celebrated Spring Apple Blossom Time three weeks earlier, at Sanborn Park.

I couldn't wait for Monday 2nd May when the children could come. When the 1st of May came, I went out and decorated my own beautiful wrought-iron May Day pole that my husband Willys had bought me. It wasn't quite tall enough, so we added an old stairway railing that we weren't using. I cut boughs from the mock orange and filled the Maypole with these branches with their white, fragrant flowers peeking out, and then I added some paper ribbons of white and apricot.

When Jenni's mother dressed in her May Day Queen gown arrived, she joined us in picture-taking around the Maypole under the oak in my garden. We toasted the day and our May Days ahead with champagne and laughed about the event. Then sparks of new life began to flow – why couldn't it be held at their Congress Springs Winery? They could go into the woods and bring back the pole on their shoulders, decorate it, and have a caller to call the dances. The family knew of Renaissance musicians who could play. We began to think of the food. Well, it was the birth of new adventures for all of us and we had a whole year to plan!

The next day I arrived at school with ribbons and baskets of smilax. I don't see how any household can do without this plant. I packed up the dress-ups and gathered some Spring Green paper for the tables we would find up there in the woods. The children had heard the story of the Maypole and how the Queen is chosen, and now we were on our way to the woods.

Upon reaching the woods, we found the beautiful May Day Queen near a tree waiting for us. She led us all to the Maypole. What a sight it was, with its gold and green streamers, but they had already been plaited. How beautiful it was with its decorated crown. All the woodland flowers and ferns had been used to match the ribbons. It was evident that some folks must have danced all night and left it there just for us to use.

The May Day Queen sat down on the grass and waited while we

made our garlands with the smilax and beautiful Spring-coloured ribbons that flowed down our backs. Then the children layered themselves with dress-ups. The boys put on capes, each one looking like a prince.

Just as we were ready, we heard the Piper of Spring. We had just formed a line ready to circle the Maypole, but then we heard the sound of the Piper.

Off they ran and found the piper in a tree with as many low-sitting branches as there were children. They sat and listened to him play each of his three pipes, and then in grand procession he led us to the Maypole. It is here that we bowed to the May Day Queen. And as I was unplaiting the ribbons, kissed that old hand-carved Maypole that Charles had made for the Community Garden. That pole has been part of my life's celebration. It looked so majestic against the blue sky here in the heart of this little apple orchard. The children remembered being here earlier in this new spot when the apple trees were in blossom. At that time it was Spring's first day, and we sat under them and smelled their fragrance. It was the smell of Spring. We ate our Spring Green apples, and thank-yous were given to those who had planted the trees, to the rain, to the sun, to the bees, and to everyone.

And here we were now on this May Day dancing around this Maypole on the most beautiful of days, bordered on one side by meadows and an old orchard. After each dance we would bow to the May Day Queen. The Piper then played for us on his violin. He played long sustaining notes for our bows, which were artistically beautiful in every way.

When the Maypole dancing was over, the Piper and the May Day Queen led us to the meadow. Here by the meadow was an old snowball tree. I picked two branches, and the May Day Queen held the branches in the middle of the Golden Ring. We found ourselves in a field of wild flowers – buttercups and small lupins everywhere. The first line of our song is, 'Here is a branch of snowy May'. It was a touch of magic that waited for us in this old tree with its arms of snowballs outstretched for us to gather for this particular group of children on this 2nd May in 1988. Spring Green was all around us, and I had worn my Lady Spring dress, designed with May Day dancing in mind. Roses that my dear sister had made during her last weeks before the angels gathered her up were sewn on the ribbons that circled the dress. This is the dress that was designed especially for my Alpha and Omega party, that would usher in my last Spring with the Kindergarten.

We both held the branches high as the children sang and danced:

BRANCH OF MAY

Traditional tune from Holland   Author unknown

Here's a branch of sno-wy May, a branch the fair- ies gave me.

Who would like to dance to- day, with a branch the fair- ies gave me?

Dance a- way,   dance a- way,   hold- ing high the branch of May.

Dance a- way, dance a- way, hold- ing high the branch of   May.

They danced around each one of us. This formed the lemniscates, which is our sign for infinity. The wedding ceremony long ago was sealed with this hand-clasp by the bride and groom. This meant that the marriage was for eternity. This marriage symbol was used last in Scotland.

At the end of each dance, the two children who danced together bowed to each other. We began to see how important this was, and the May Day Queen and I also bowed.

After everyone had a turn, the Piper again took his pipe and piped us over to the redwood circle. Here we stood among the giant redwood trees, finding one that had been made into a throne just right for the May Day Queen. As she sat there, we all called to her like doves – then owls, then woodpeckers, then quail.

Now it was time to wave goodbye to the piper, and then we turned to the May Day Queen to thank her. Each child was called up to thank the Queen. Each one bowed his most majestic bow, and some of the boys knelt on one knee. Eric took his garland off and flourished it in the air before his bow. The magic of May had settled into all of us – adults and children alike.

My thank-yous to all of you who made this day possible. How wonderful to be able to draw on the memory of this experience when we celebrated May Day together in the woods. May all Kindergartens everywhere know the importance of a May Day celebration.

We have known the feeling of meadows; we have seen with our eyes the May Day Queen; we have heard the Piper of Spring; we have danced and we have sung our songs under sunlit blue skies; and we have felt a sense of royalty in our majestic bowing to the Queen as we stood enclosed by symbols of great strength, the redwood trees, in a glen of quietness and of strength, where our souls can touch and be forever renewed by the spirit that dwells mysteriously in all things.

The following year, our Kindergarten decided to cut down the eucalyptus tree that we had watch grow from a pod that someone had dropped in our sandbox. It had grown straight up. Billy's father came to help us not only cut it down, but strip it. We all helped. The leaves were saved for our many activities, and the tree was placed in position by a neighbour across the street from our classroom.

The ribbons arrived just in time for our May Day dancing celebration at our own school with our own home-grown Maypole. I now own three Maypoles.

Mother's Day

The celebration of Mother's Day at the age of five is a celebration of life itself. With this realization in mind, an outpouring of love finds its way into all our activities to celebrate this day.

Our writing becomes a vehicle of love. I have for many years got the children to write 'I love you' on little pieces of paper, some all decorated with Spring. These are taken home and hidden in secret places throughout their house. They delight in telling where they are going to hide them. Some say, 'In her shoe'. Others say, 'Under her pillow', and so on.

Mothers have told me how thrilling it is to find these treasures everywhere. The gift-giving is a vital necessity of the day. To be able to give the highest of all true gifts means to give from the heart. A true gift means to have found the greatest gesture of love in its simplest form. A gift that will bring a surprise tug at the heart is always a joy. To discover a gift in a chosen secret hiding-place gives the giver and receiver an exchange of ecstasy! This simple gesture of hiding 'I love yous' is worthy of the position of a true gift. In addition, we make a formal permanent gift. We use water colours to paint a flowering vine as a border. This now forms a frame for the 'I love you' words that we write in gold. We sign our names in silver – these are always delightful enough to frame and keep for ever.

Every petal from the flowers that enter the Kindergarten room is saved. In the garden outside our door the children gather the flowers that are 'trying to get back to Mother Earth'. These petals are added to our basket of potpourri. Just before Mother's Day, we find the large basket is full to overflowing. There is always lots of lavender and mint, to which we add a drop of rose oil. The children sit around the basket and pick out which petals will be theirs, to be placed in our potpourri bags. So they are twice-picked flowers. We choose two colours of Spring ribbon to tie them.

On Wednesday, our cookie time, finds us making two M's, 'one for Mum and one for Me'. These M's are decorated with a maraschino cherry, and cut and assembled by the designer himself. They will be wrapped for a special gift.

When we returned from our May Day in the apple orchard, we made a book of our activities. These books were so lovely, telling about the Maypole dancing, the Piper of Spring, and our visit to the meadow filled with wild flowers, that I decided to give them as gifts. I, too, cherished that special May Day and wrote a detailed description, which was tucked inside each book. The teacher's words that go home must ring with insight, wisdom, and understanding of the development of the child. Lucky is the parent who has the kind of teacher who sends notes home so that the parents can feel a vital part of the class. How often I have felt guilty when time jams up and I scratch a note home with vital information, but no food for the soul.

After our gifts were made, the children wrote an invitation: 'Come, 10:30, 8th May'. Each invitation is an opportunity to display our artistic skills. It is at this time on Mother's Day that we celebrate Spring with all its poetry, songs, and dance for our mothers. Some time ago I discovered that if I sent the poem or song home, the whole household became involved. The surprise element was overshadowed by the keen interest of the family, who were all learning it. Of course we had been saying them all in Kindergarten since Lady Spring arrived, so in Kindergarten we never have a practice. After we choose which songs or poems we will use for our celebration, we organize our places.

Our Mother's Day is always held in the garden. Only once did we have to move inside because of rain. On the morning of this year's event we decorated our places and gathered dress-ups for our costumes. Everyone, of course, knew everyone's part, so there was no concern about forgetting. You could always ask someone to say it with you if you thought you would forget. As the mothers arrived, they were given gifts we had made for them to wear. These gifts were crowns of garlands made of smilax, with flowers from our garden tucked in.

The children look like flowers themselves, all scattered about the garden. At this time I wear the colour blue – the colour of motherhood. This deep feeling for the colour blue was captured by the great masters of our Western art long ago in their paintings of mothers. It is a colour chosen wisely to which we all respond as a nourishing, peaceful colour – the sky, the sea, the ever-enfolding calm, and the great rumbling of the thunder, the great tossing of the sea. The finding of calm must be ours, to balance out all of life. And as I look around at our guests, I see that this ancient symbolism still lives today: every mother seems to be wearing blue.

When all is in order, I stand to welcome them all. When I look into these beautiful young mothers' faces, my eyes fill with tears. Such expectation, joy, and love fill their eyes. There is something about working with mothers that brings one a vital sense of the hope for the future, a sense that everything will be all right, everything will balance out. Here it is, motherhood at its finest hour.

I remember looking at Lee Anne and saying, 'Lee Anne will play some Mother's Day music before we begin'. As she serenades us with her beautiful violin music, it gives me time to shed my tears of joy for being a part of this magic which fills the air when mother and child hold the world in their hands and heart, and with unseen golden threads hold it high for the gods to bless.

Our story for the week was Cinderella. Before each child is introduced, I introduce the Fairy Godmothers. Each family is responsible for sending a Fairy Godmother if the mother in the family cannot come. Lee, the good neighbour and friend of Brian's family, had come several weeks before to express her concern about Mother's Day with Brian. This would be his first Mother's Day without her – she had died of cancer the previous year. We decided then and there that she would dress as a Fairy Godmother and come to be his Fairy Godmother for the celebration.

I had told Brian that the office would call us when his Fairy Godmother arrived. Everyone was looking forward to hearing her entrance announced. When the call came from our 'listening ear', we both hurried to the office to greet her. There she stood, dressed in a long, white gown. (I later learned that it was the gown she wore when she was chosen to be the Queen at her college.) She also was wearing not only wings but a royal headpiece and carrying a star wand. I later learned that Brian's dad had carved it out of wood for her.

John's mother could not be there that day. His Fairy Godmother arrived with wings, a star wand, and a crown. I can't tell you how important it is for a child to fall into the loving arms of a mother, grandmother, or Fairy Godmother at a time like this. Woe be to the mother who neglects these moments in this ongoing process of turning sons and daughters into loving parents for the next generation.

After the Fairy Godmothers has been introduced, each child in the Kindergarten is then introduced. The introduction is enhanced with a bow, not just any bow, but a bow that contains all of the child's relationships with himself and how he feels about this moment. It is a gesture that means many things on many levels: his recognition of others as well as himself; his training in bowing from dance teachers, karate teachers, and music teachers. His lessons in bowing from his father are also seen, as well as his grasp of entertainers bowing. His feel for a sense of history comes through in presenting his bow. This gracious acknowledgement of his role as a student, entertainer, son or daughter, and individual with great worth sparkles, as this timeless gesture of gratitude is returned to the teacher and the audience when his name is spoken. There are many opportunities in our Kindergarten to perfect the art of bowing, especially after your gift of poetry or song is given.

First, the children who are King and Queen of May welcome everyone. Then the one chosen to be the Sun rises before our eyes, saying his Sun poem. The Moon then grows into a full face while we all sing, and Lady Spring dances to her poetry. Then the Flower Queen is helped from under the ground by two gnomes, ascending her throne as she scatters the woods and fields with flowers. Then comes the Piper of Spring, calling all the little wild things – the rabbits, bees, and butterflies – to him. It is Mother Earth who then calls the seeds, and Phoebe has her turn to be the Snowbell, wearing a white snowbell hat her mother made for the occasion. Then Little Johnny Jump Up says his poem. Each year we grow flowers in our garden to match our poems, and the children delight in dressing in the colours of these flowers.

Then comes the moment when we celebrate the rainbow. This is where the rain and the sun perform together as the 'arch of rainbow spans the sky'. All of science, number work, ecology, literature, music, and dance are woven into this programme under the sycamore trees in our beautiful garden.

In order to gather the children up, I sing my song in memory of my mother. My mother was a lover of meadows and flowers. She loved the outdoors, and we were always with her. The teacher who has shared the class all year walks with me as we sing.

As I sing, I gather the children and we walk together until we are again facing the parents. At this time we say the poem about every creature loving to feel their mothers' hug:

Every baby, bird, and bee,
Every squirrel in the tree,
Every butterfly and bug
Loves to feel his mother's hug.

Author unknown

As the children tumble into their mothers' arms, I take our decorated hoops of crepe paper and flowers and call a child with his mother to come and hold the hoops as they dance around under the sycamore tree:

MOTHER, OH MOTHER

Betty Peck

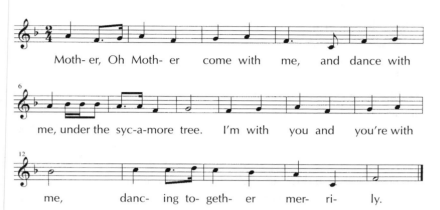

Moth-er, Oh Moth-er come with me, and dance with me, under the syc-a-more tree. I'm with you and you're with me, danc-ing to-geth-er mer-ri-ly.

When every mother and child has had a turn holding on to the hoops and dancing, we two teachers take the ends of a long piece of blue silk and poof it into the sky. It fills with air, forming a majestic arch for each mother and her child to walk through. Chip's mother took the blue silk home and added stars, constellations, and our own Milky Way. As mother and child are called in turn to enter through this gate that silkworms have prepared to hold air and sky, they step into the redwood area. We have a tall redwood tree that stands like a mother with her arms outstretched, shadowing our redwood tree table. The table has been decorated with cloths and flowers, and it is here where the mums find their handmade gifts all wrapped for a surprise opening. Michelle, the Sound Party Queen for the week, has brought maple ice cream cones for us all. All the mothers eat their 'M' cookies, smell their Mother's Day gifts of rose petals, see in gold their children's 'I love you', and open their child's May Day Memory Book.

Honour women:
They entwine and weave the roses of heaven
Into the life we live on earth.

Schiller

Father's Day

This celebration of father takes place in my own garden. A note has been sent home many months before, asking the fathers to keep this date free. If necessary, I offer to write a letter to their employer, asking for permission to have this day declared a holiday for this father and his child. A grandfather, uncle, or friend of the family comes with the child if there is no father in the family.

Our special story for Father's Day is 'The Donkey' from the Brothers Grimm. We make crowns for our fathers which they are given to wear on this special day. Our gift of our alphabet book that we have made over the year is hidden in the garden by the child and together they find it and read its contents. Then we line up according to our father's gift to us; our last name. The last initial of the family name is designed in an outdoor plaque made with nails we hammer into wood.

We think of all the things that our fathers would like to do: play in the creek, ride the train, sing and dance, and eat. Together the children and I plan the day. The singing game will be 'The Noble Duke of York' and 'The King Loved Me So'. I always give a little talk about my own father. The children always ask if we can start the celebration the same way we start each day in the Golden Ring.

There are never enough songs for Father's Day, so I wrote this one:

THE KING LOVED ME SO

Directions: The child chosen to be the father stands in the middle with a chosen daughter on one side and a chosen son on the other side, and they skip around the circle. On the chorus, they stop and the two children crouch down and slowly grow up with their father's hand on their head as the chorus is sung. First the daughter, and then the son.

> The King loved me so –
> That he greeted me each morning
> In the royal way, in the royal way!
> > *REFRAIN:*
> > And I grew up, and I grew up to be a prince.
> > And I grew up, and I grew up to be a princess.

THE KING LOVED ME SO

Betty Peck

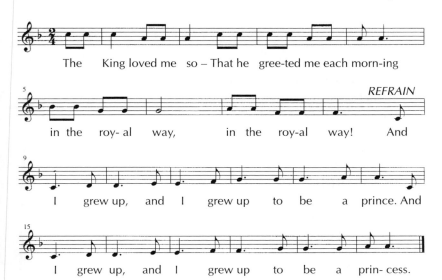

The King loved me so – That he greeted me each morning
in the royal way, in the royal way!

The King loved me so –
That he taught me the rules,
The very royal rules, the very royal rules!
   REFRAIN
The King loved me so –
That we went on walks
Through the royal woods, through the royal woods!
   REFRAIN
The King loved me so –
That he taught me each day
How to be polite, how to be polite!
   REFRAIN
The King loved me so –
That he showed me the way,
The very royal way, the very royal way!
   REFRAIN

The King loved me so –
That he told me he did
Every royal day, every royal day!
 REFRAIN
The King loved me so –
That he built the walls high
Around the royal Kingdom, around the royal Kingdom.
 REFRAIN
The King loved me so –
That he taught me how to bow
In the royal way, in the royal way!
 REFRAIN
The King loved me so –
That he gave me his promise,
A very royal promise, a very royal promise.
 REFRAIN
The King loved me so –
That we talked together
Every royal day, every royal day!
 REFRAIN
The King loved me so –
That he wrote me a poem
With the royal pen, with the royal pen!
 REFRAIN
The King loved me so –
That he smiles at me,
A very royal smile, a very royal smile.
 REFRAIN
The King loved me so –
That he read to me
All the royal books, all the royal books!
 REFRAIN
The King loved me so –
That he asked me each day
How I helped the Queen, how I helped the Queen!
 REFRAIN
The King loved me so –
That he watched my manners

In the royal way, in the royal way!
  REFRAIN
The King loved me so –
That together we polished
All the royal shoes, all the royal shoes!
  REFRAIN
The King loved me so –
That together we always worked
In the royal garden, in the royal garden!
  REFRAIN
The King loved me so –
That he always had a joke
In his royal pocket, in his royal pocket!
  REFRAIN
The King loved me so –
That he took me for a drive
In the royal coach, in the royal coach!
  REFRAIN
The King loved me so –
That he worked hard each day
In the royal way, in the royal way!
  REFRAIN
The King loved me so –
That he gave me a tutor
A very royal tutor, a very royal tutor.
  REFRAIN
The King loved me so –
That he played for me
On the royal pipes, on the royal pipes.
  REFRAIN
The King loved me so –
That he blew out the light
And said a royal good night, and said a royal good night!
  REFRAIN

Celebrating Birthdays

Celebration Letter home to parents

Dears,

The need for celebration is a vital part of the fabric of the human spirit. Anticipation is a powerful pulling together of the life forces in the role of celebration: it gives strength to the imagination, sharpens the ability to focus on the essence of the forthcoming event, deepens our sense of gratitude to all the forces making the event possible.

All parents sense the joy that children have in looking forward to their birthdays. How many days until I celebrate my birthday? How shall we celebrate? There are many steps leading up to this moment, such as family histories connecting the child to his/her roots. There may be pre-birthday surprise gifts tucked away that are only found by following a yarn path or reading a note written by some beloved toy that tells where the gift is hidden. Stretching out the anticipation builds their focus and joy of living and fills our days with gratitude.

By celebrating the rhythmic flow of the year, the seasons, the week, the day gives structure and order to our lives, and provides strength that is needed to rise above all the yin and yang, the swing between joy and sorrow that is needed for our aliveness. What special days mark your family's year? How do you honour the seasons? Does your week have a balance of activity and rest? How does your day flow?

Are there times set aside to celebrate the first rainfall, a rainbow sighting, the full moon, a loose tooth, all the intimate, unique moments that belong to your family? How do we celebrate the human spirit? Once when I was being honoured, a former Kindergarten student who was now a senior in high school came to speak. Kirsten started her speech by saying, 'Celebrate, celebrate, celebrate, in Kindergarten we learned to celebrate'. Then she went on to recall how the Piper of Spring had come to our Kindergarten, and that they had heard his music as he piped up and down the garden pathways, and all ran out of the door to meet him.

Because of the poem we had learned, 'There Piped a Piper in the Woods', the children knew he was part of Spring. In the weeks before, the children had learned the poem and now he had arrived. Throughout the year such visitors had come. People we had met through stories, verses, and songs.

Heralds and characters of each season that are the stepping stones of our lives. We were not going to let Santa be the only messenger. Each celebration is always wrapped in its own colourful decorations, music, stories, food, poetry, and ceremony – the simpler the better. This artistic expansion helps to nourish our senses. The enrichment of our senses provides the fundamental aura of our lives.

Now, as a grandmother, I have the luxury of continuing to celebrate wonder. I am able to play a magical role in the lives of my grandchildren and to share with them the enchanting realm of elves, fairies, gnomes, and angels. All of which is so close to the heart of childhood and where they long to live.

Sarah and Merina each have a fairy mailbox in the olive tree and an old oak stump in different parts of the garden which hold their letters and answers which their fairies write. Last evening when my grandchildren arrived, there was a lighted fairy candle on the steps that shone on a letter written by the fairies. The children had asked for fairy wings. Well, said the note, 'fairies grow their own wings'. However, the note, on beautiful sparkling paper, said, 'We have decided that your wings had to be substantial, yet airy and light. So here they are for your imaginations to fly around in'. And so we took flashlights and started through the garden looking for them. Of course not everyone believes in fairies. Isn't it interesting that, at this moment in the heart of Silicon Valley, our own belief in fairies was being given credence by the newly released movie, 'Fairytale – A True Story'?

I celebrate the mysteries of life! My philosophy as well as my philosophy of teaching is the CELEBRATION of life!

Hugs,

bp

One of our favourite old clapping nursery rhymes is:

Apples, pears, peaches, and plums,
Show me when your birthday comes.
   [They tell me the date and point.]
Apples, pears, peaches, and plums,
Tell me what season of the year your birthday comes.
   [They name the season.]
Apples, pears, peaches, and plums,
Tell me the number of the month your birthday comes.
   [They name the number of the month.]

Apples, pears, peaches, and plums,
Show me when your birthday comes.
   [They go to the Birthday Boards and find their date of birth.]

There is nothing the child comes to school with that is more important to her than her birthday. There is true magic in this day of all days.... On growing through the years with my own children, it seemed too long to wait for a whole year, so we celebrated their half-birthdays. As they grew older, it was hard to give up this custom, and perhaps they never have.

The celebration of the Kindergarten birthday has evolved over many years. When the orchards grew all around us, we had a birthday tree out in the orchard. We took out all our birthday necessities and the birthday child sat in the fork of the prune tree while the others made a fairy ring around the tree, wearing mustard garlands when it was winter. In spring they wore blossoms. We always hung large cardboard prunes in the tree; if the child turned five, there were five prunes.

Now that the orchards have disappeared, we celebrate this special day in our classroom. But our garden still sings 'Happy Birthday' to the birthday child. The garden is filled with fives (rosaceae) and sixes (liliaceae). The apple has five little beds for its seeds that make the star inside the apple. The strawberry has five little green fingers holding on to this bright red treasure house of Mother Earth's. The tomato has its green hand, with its five fingers holding it on the silver cord. The daffodil has its six petals.... So in our Kindergarten, the child feels the whole earth is celebrating his special day.

We celebrate birthdays inside our Kindergarten classroom the very first day the children enter the Kindergarten. On this first day the child stays for only 20 minutes with a small group of children, and he is asked, 'When's your birthday?'. At this time his birthday is placed within the context of the whole year on the birthday boards, which the child can see stretched out along the wall. His birth date is visible all year long for all to see, and he is known as the Birthday Child weeks before his birthday arrives. 'The Birthday Boy may do the counting'. 'The Birthday Girl will lead the parade.' 'The Birthday Boy will be Mother Earth.' This clears the air for the others, for they know their turn will come. Never will there be a birthday time just like this one of turning five or six. We as adults spend our lives trying to capture the essence of this period of time when the world was new and we were filled with awe.

On the day of the child's birthday, the Kindergarten friends hurry around and decorate a small table, at which there are two chairs. They always look beautiful, no matter how many scarves and veils the children use, and on both chairs is a golden crown, with a star wand laid on one of them.

So there are two chairs, yes, two chairs, at the birthday table – one for the Birthday Child and one for the Guardian Angel. Years ago I wanted to enlarge birthday parties to include more than just the focus of the Birthday Child; and the Guardian Angel has been the perfect answer. Everyone wants to be chosen for this honoured place. It is she who holds the star wand and leads the child down from the heavens.

Cupcakes are placed along the edge of the table, with much counting and licking of fingers. Someone is chosen to bring five flowers in from the garden, which are put into five chosen vases. The vases form a circle in the middle of the birthday table – we've learned through experience not to fill them with water. Then the rainbow is made from the table to the highest cloud in the room, which happens to be our two-storey playhouse that was built in the corner of the room. Rainbow-coloured materials are placed in proper order on the floor. I wish the children always to identify this day with all the beauty that we can bring to the celebration. Rainbows hold such a major place in a child's heart that they cannot be left out of the ceremony. As you know, they resonate with the order of the universe .

I remember when on one occasion, Scott was painting rainbows, and his rainbows somehow got connected to a cloud. He looked up and said, 'Oh! Is that how people get to heaven?' Anyway, our rainbow is all ready for the Guardian Angel with her star wand to lead the Birthday Child to the earth.

The day would not be complete without a birthday banner to herald the event. This banner hangs in its special place all year, waiting for birthdays. It is then that it is taken down from its place and given its proper setting. This banner was designed by one of my most artistic mothers, Karen and Dean's mum – students from long ago who are now both artists themselves (the birthright of every educated person). This banner is made of appliqued cotton of bright colours with a background of red. There you see symbolic figures of marionettes dancing among the numbers five, six, and seven with their strings visible. Little did she know how many children this banner would honour.

This banner is hung to the side, and the child's own birthday poem is hung in the centre spot, on a large sheet of paper, making it the main focus. I write a special short poem for every child's birthday; the poem must be carefully suited to the child in every way, for we shall soon say it all together and take it home for our own walls.

Some Sample Birthday Poems

> I walk quietly along the path
> With my shining heart of gold
> That will be with me even when I am old.

> Stars shine on me,
> Giving me joy
> When I help all I see.

The purpose of these poems is to focus on the positive gift that each child brings. It is here on this day that the teacher sets the tone for the celebration through words as well as decor.

A special place has been prepared for the family of the Birthday Child. The adults are given small finger cymbals to ring, and the sound of the cymbals helps fill the room with music when 'thank-yous' are said. I want the children to know the magic and the beauty of a thank-you. This playing of the cymbals to accompany the 'thank-yous' makes it easy to remember how important these words are. I remember saying to the children of a long ago Kindergarten, 'When you say "thank you", I hear beautiful bells ringing'. Then I thought, why not let the children hear them also? I now have a collection of small bells and cymbals that are used for these special occasions.

When all is ready for the birthday party, the children are called in from play, with the Birthday Child entering last of all. They all come in hoping to be the Guardian Angel – it is such a special role. First, however, everyone is given a page that will go into the child's birthday book, on which they each draw a picture of themselves. A small table covered with cloths is set beside the Birthday Child so that she will have a place to put these gifts. This book will be bound together to take home after the celebration.

After the Birthday Child chooses the Guardian Angel and the pictures are drawn, the A. A. Milne poem 'When I Am Six' is recited to set the stage: this is a poem I know from my childhood, and I tell the story each time about the father who wrote this poem for his little boy long ago. 'When I was one, I had just begun', and so on.

I tell the children how important birthday poems are and that I always feel good getting poems for my birthday. This is why I have written a birthday poem for today's Birthday Child. This poem has been hung up on the wall, and we stand and say the verse together with its accompanying gestures.

In order to tell how many times the birthday child has gone around the sun, I hold in my hand five long stems of lavender that grows outside our door to represent five years. The birthday child's hand is placed in mine, and we begin our journey around the sun. As we go, we sing a beautiful song written by my daughter, Anna Rainville:

ONE, TWO, THREE, FOUR, FIVE

Anna Rainville

One, two, three, four, five. Five jour-neys 'round the sun, Through the win-ter, spring and

sum-mer, and fall, I jour-ney 'round the sun. My new year has be- gun.

At the end of the verse, which we sing five times if the child is five years old, I give the child one of the lavender stems to place in one of the five vases each time we journey round the Birthday table. The others look to see each time how many are left.

Once while we were singing, Kim put our big sun (which we wear for Father Sun that Tim's mother made) under the table so that we would truly go round the sun. Since then I have put it there myself, now that she is no longer in Kindergarten.

When this part of the ceremony is finished, the Birthday Child and the Guardian Angel go up the stairs to the highest part of the sky and look down to see whom the child will choose for his parents. I want the children to feel as though they are looking down over the earth for the first time and choosing the very best of all parents for themselves. When we first see the child's face look through the upstairs windows in our corner playhouse, we all sing 'Happy Birthday'.

After the song, the Guardian Angel with a star wand guides the child down and across the rainbow trail to his place at the table.

Now is the time for him to choose his friends, one at a time, to come up and get a cupcake. They come up and say, 'Happy Birthday, Alicia', and she says, 'Thank you'. And the chimes ring. 'Please help yourself', she says. Then it is their turn to say, 'Thank you for the cup-cake'. And the chimes ring.

Childhood means your birthday is the day of days. When I was very young, on one of my 'day of days', I remember the doors of the den being thrown open and seeing that the den had been transformed into a bedroom for me with a new French bedroom set, lamps, linens, carpets... everything that would make one a queen forever. My grandmother, who was always filled with poetry and stories, had given this gift to me with the help of the whole family. To this day, I shall never know how they kept it a secret from me until my 'day of days'. I wish for all children to be able to look back on their birthdays with the same joy and ecstasy I felt on that special day.

Then there comes a time on your birthday when you acknowledge your existence with a turn to the founders of the feast itself. Soon your gratitude for the existence of life itself which you possess transforms into a new relationship with those who have made it all possible.

I am still celebrating my gratefulness for having been born, and so I gather together my class and their parents to celebrate my birthday. I have spent the year celebrating their birthdays, and now they are invited to celebrate mine on the 18th of December. I have a different ceremony for my birthday. I wish to bring the children closer to me, and to take the children to my home. I like the children to understand that because I am an adult, I am able to help my Guardian Angel. Children are not little adults. Adults, I feel, have become more able to help their own Guardian Angels.

At Kindergarten we hang stars from the ceiling, which are pictures of the children – for each child is a star. Now on my birthday we will be *under* the stars, the real stars. This is why we go up on the rooftop deck at my house. The children are given an apple representing their life, with a candle in it to represent their own inner divine spark. I have a very large candle, and as I stand in the middle of the circle under the stars, I call each one up, lighting their lives with my candle. But when I look at this shining circle of light, I realize it is my life that is shining from their glowing candles. 'We are the most wonderful Kindergarten under the stars'; of course we say this in our schoolroom too, but now we say it under the night sky filled with stars.

On this occasion I also get to see the children with both their parents. The family is what Christmas is all about. No siblings are allowed at this event: It is the child's night to come as the great triangle of strength – child, mother, father.

We always eat first when celebrating my birthday. Then we gather in the Great Hall (our indoor 'theatre') for the telling of a special story. The telling of this story is always a nourishing experience for me, looking into the faces of the families gathered in front of the great fireplace. Here they sit, all beautifully dressed, angelic, nestled in the arms of their parents, entrusting themselves to us, their teachers. Every gathering should be blessed with a story in the Kindergarten.

When the candle is lit, I sing 'Mother of the Fairy Tale', and the story begins. I love to tell the story of 'The Loaf of Bread' – a story that tells how important it is to share what we have with others. After the story has ended, each child takes her apple with the candle inside it up to the rooftop deck. As we stand under the stars, we hear the bell toll my years, as we count aloud each year. Memories of each age flood my soul. I believe that the ritual of counting should be established on all birthdays – all the years of your life can be conjured up to connect you to your steps into the future.

I have wonderful memories of standing in the middle with the large candle and calling each one up to light their candle. This is the teacher's responsibility and joy – to create an environment so that their light may shine. As I call them up one by one to light their candles, I hope never to forget that I now am standing in a brighter light that could never be possible without them. I myself learn more from them than it is ever possible for them to learn from me. It is here that I look into the eyes of the future. Here is *the future!*

As we stand under the stars, we feel them shining down, helping us realize that we are formed of stardust! The starlight, sparkling in their eyes from the candlelight, is a treasure that only we as teachers can feel – the true meaning of this mystery, the mystery of the teacher and the student. The miracle of learning to trust someone outside the home, the transferring of the trust of mother and father to the teacher, is a miracle in itself. Nothing needs to be said at this time, and I am often quite overcome by the moment.

After reciting the verse that my mother taught me as a child at this time of year: *'And there were shepherds in the same country abiding in the field, and keeping watch by night'*, we sing our parents a lullaby:

> The flowers nod.
> The shadows creep.
> A shadow comes over the hill.
> The little lambs have gone to sleep,
> The little birds are still.
> The world is full of drowsy things
> And soft with candlelight.
> The nests are full of folded wings.
> Goodnight, goodnight, goodnight.
>
> Author unknown

Then they are on their way home, after singing 'Happy Birthday' to me, which always comes as a surprise, as everything we have done that evening is a Happy Birthday.

Summer Birthdays

How does one handle the birthdays of children who were born in summer? Every teacher must find her own meaningful way. Windows framed our catalpa tree on one side of the Kindergarten room. We literally *lived* in this tree! It dramatically announced the seasons: In early September when the children arrived, the leaves were green, changing rapidly to gold by the end of November; during the winter months the tree stands bare. Is it dead? We were not sure or given any promise at all till the first sign of Spring burst through with the uncurling of its new leaves in March – the whole tree turned Spring-green.

This cycle of the tree was recorded by our class and announced to the entire school through our drawings, our paintings, and our dictated illustrated stories. I had never lived with a catalpa tree before; this tree had never been a part of my life. The children and I would marvel at the way in which the tree would know what our classroom needed most during the year. It gave us the gift of shade in late summer with its large leaves. When these leaves returned to Mother Earth, the best of the winter light poured in through the windows. Just when we all needed new life after the winter months, the tree announced to all that it was not dead and new life surged through its branches, and into all of us.

This would have been enough to ask of any tree, but then, to our surprise, white blossoms a foot long appeared the first of June – of course it was announcing summer. And with summer come summer birthdays – what better time to celebrate these birthdays? The colour scheme is already provided with white blossoms and spring-green leaves.

It was easy to decide that we should all wear white. We gathered all the white flowers, and each flower family had its own vase. Invitations had to be made to invite the parents – these were illustrated with motifs of the catalpa tree. The word 'come' and the time were written on Spring-green paper that matched the new leaves. Each Birthday Child set up his own table with two chairs decorated with white paper. The other children painted large pictures of the blossoming tree to be hung on the outside walls. The Birthday Children painted pictures of themselves to be pinned to large art screens that made the area under the catalpa tree quite a private setting for the party.

When the parents were seated, the procession of SINGING children dressed in white, carrying vases of white flowers, came down the path under the tree. This path had been decorated with white crepe-paper flowers on portable columns that we had made. Each child wore a catalpa tree hat with white flowers from the tree. The flowers were placed on the birthday tables and on the serving table that had been decorated for the occasion.

We sang our spring songs and danced our singing games. Then the Birthday Children with their Guardian Angel sat at their tables while the others sat with their parents. The Kindergarten birthday celebration began. After the children ate their cup-cakes, there was home-made vanilla ice cream for everyone.

Never, never miss the opportunity to enrich lives through

celebration. It will always be a joyous occasion if the arts permeate every level of the celebration in a simple, meaningful, and elegant way.

Tooth Fairy Celebration

Nothing is more important to the Kindergarten child than losing a tooth – the whole family is centred on this event. The entire Kindergarten is involved in this occasion that announces to the world that he is now ready for new adventures. He can now feel his own growth with the losing of a tooth. This is one of his first big bodily changes that says 'goodbye' to babyhood. To the educator, as Rudolf Steiner so clearly pointed out, this means that the child is now ready to take his first steps into abstract learning. From now on, there will be room for symbolic learning. How does the teacher celebrate this event?

My most meaningful way is when the Tooth Fairy herself finds her way to our room. On that day we all wear our pyjamas and nightgowns. We have cleaned our nests and spread our blankets out. As we lie on our rugs listening for some signals, she has arrived. The whole room is darkened when we hear the news from our Listening Ear that the Tooth Fairy has arrived. Down from the long hallway we hear her singing lullabies. Lullabies are the only songs she knows, for her work is always at night when she comes to the houses of children who have lost their teeth. As she enters our room, she sprinkles stardust on all the children. They lie so still as they listen to her songs and feel the star-shine on their skin.

Sometimes in our Kindergarten, the Tooth Fairy brings a little fairy who is learning to be a Tooth Fairy. Only the real Tooth Fairy wears wings, but they both carry wands. The children hear them talk to each other. When she has covered all the children with stardust, the Tooth Fairy sees her lovely white throne that reaches up to the stars. She then sits down and calls the children's names whom she knows, for she has visited them while they slept to leave her gift under their pillow in exchange for their tooth.

We have prepared individual tables (tree stumps) covered with white gossamer (curtains), and on the table are small dishes. Beside each tea table covered in white is a little chair for each child who has lost a tooth. As the Tooth Fairy calls each child's name, they leave their resting rug where they have been waiting for their name to be called and find a seat at one of the little tea tables. The children who haven't lost their teeth are the servants: they pour the tea and serve cookies to the children and the Tooth Fairy and the little fairy. They pour tea into our small tea cups made by Rachael and her mother, that I still use for the Kindergarten teachers.

Each servant sits beside the one she is serving, and they eat together. As they eat, the Tooth Fairy asks if they have any questions? 'Where do you live?'. She answers, 'Behind the farthest star'. Then comes the magic light that the Tooth Fairy holds in her hand. I want to see when I shall be coming to see you. Then she holds the little fairy light up to the child who hasn't yet lost a tooth. They show her the ones that are loose and she says, 'Soon I will come'.

Then she puts her hand on their cheeks and says, 'When you are sleeping, this is the way I say "thank you" for your "gift" to me, your little ivory tooth'.

The Tooth Fairy is always the most beautiful of all fairies – she wears a white gown with pink ribbons. On her head is a diamond tiara. The little fairy wears a pink gown and carries her wand. They sing together more lullabies as they leave the room, and we sing our 'thank you' song to her.

PART V

Activity and Early Learning

Early Literacy Experience

In our Kindergarten, large golden wooden letters of the alphabet are placed high up on our walls among the stars. The children must stand on a chair to reach them. These, of course, are the 'upper-case letters'. They received their name 'upper-case' from their location on the printer's supply stand of long ago.

All teachers cannot help but see in their mind's eye as they teach these capital letters, the beautifully inscribed Roman letters on the columns and capitals in Rome. Every presentation of the letters is in historical order: first the capital is presented and then the small letters.

Letter Writing

All Kindergarten children bring into Kindergarten their own secret writing code that they have used since they could first hold a pencil. But comes the day when they realize that the sounds of our English language have been given homes within the form of the 26 letters of the alphabet. Then children are eager to learn how to write. Then they must know, of course, that no letter should be written without knowing the direction the letter must take – down from the stars into the hand of man.

First we draw the earth line on our paper. The letters do not grow up like flowers from the earth line; they are gifts from the stars, and they follow the starlit path down to the earth line of our paper. Stars hang from the ceiling over this portion of the room when we study our letters that hold our sounds.

Knowing the alphabetical roots of these 26 letters helps us not only to teach, but to stand in awe when we learn of our rich inheritance that we take so casually.

If anyone has ever seen a great calligrapher take his block brush and, onto a sheet of white paper, make the letter 'A', the Alpha, one knows what a religious experience is. It is a whole religious experience to see the master calligrapher bring forth his creation. His love for the form of the letter flows through every fibre of his being, and streams out to all who witness man making these letters that have been reduced from pictures, these letters that were once pictures that everyone understood. These strange lines now looked almost demonic. It was then that their meaning had to be taught.

A new era had dawned. This left everyone in need of understanding what these lines meant. It became a holy experience to dip pen in ink and pen words on parchment. One became like a mother lion who licks her cubs into life itself, creating the form. So we learn in every way to bring the shape to life.

If possible, the children see a stretched piece of parchment on a frame with the sheep's wool still attached to the borders. It is then that they realize that the sheep gave up their lives for this moment when words were first set down.

Writing was so holy that the Hebrew scribes were dressed in white, as the words were written in silence and prayer. When you look at these ancient manuscripts that are now kept under lock and key in our libraries across the world, you know what it means to be privileged to teach five-or six-year-olds to form these letters. The letters truly are gifts from the stars.

One day our faculty had the privilege to watch Daniel Bittleston, a form-drawing authority, draw a straight line on the chalkboard. A feeling of awe fell over everyone at the perfection of that straight line. Then we watched as he drew the curve. The truth is simple: All lines are straight lines and curved lines in our universe.

There before us on the chalkboard we are presented with the introduction to letter forms, the straight line and the curve. Before our eyes we see the powerful symbols of the male and female forms – the great opposites, the roots of all written forms.... All things are all things.

With every letter goes a gesture. However, it turns out to be more an entire choreographed dance. When learning the straight line gesture of 'l', we hold our hands high above our heads toward the sun and begin with the word 'summer'. Then as we let our hands fall, we say 'fall'. Then into winter snows, putting our hands on the earth. Then up into spring, and the cycle begins all over again. This is the life-line of the year.

When one is part of this destiny of pulling the line and curve into the five-or six-year-old, one feels the power, majesty, and beauty that bring the forms into being as one hands the torch to a new generation.

Each letter comes in historic picture form in the Kindergarten down to the earth line and starting from the left in our English language, where the great source of light and meaning appears. Theatre also feels this descending quality of importance known as 'stage left'.

The school year starts in autumn, so it is in autumn that the letters are tied to this season of the year. Leaves have fallen. It is now that letter 'L' / 'l' is presented. The first letter to fall from the stars in my Kindergarten is the 'L' / 'l'. The beautiful whisper of love comes down; it comes down and stays. It is a picture of myself standing on the earth. Then we draw a little earth line to show the direction along the path that we will take to carry our love to everyone. This is the same direction all English letters will take – left to right.

All of our lessons are gifts from Mother Earth. It is she who gives meaning to our Kindergarten year. We have only to open our door into our garden to find the lessons of the day.

In September the leaves fall. The California laurel outside of our door gives its leaves for us to feel and smell. This straight noble symbol of man himself (lower case L) is found as the lifeline for every leaf.

From this day on, we are lovers of leaves. They live in our schoolroom in all ways. These leaves have given us our first lesson, and those around us have no idea how important they are to us. They are often swept away before we have time to claim them as our own, for no one seems to understand their relationship to the total experience of reading and writing and learning for the young child.

This important position of the left is in relationship to our heart. This upper left-hand corner of our paper is never again overlooked in the Kindergarten. From now on, we put a little heart or 'L' as a symbol in the left hand corner to remind us that our hearts full of love have made this writing possible.

The upper-case letter 'L' points the way to proceed along the page. The children often clasp the paper to their hearts to show how their left side, which is the resting place for their hearts, matches their paper placement of the 'L'.

After the presentation of the letter on Monday, our first day of the week, we have five days of celebration of the letter. The king or queen of the week is chosen. We go around the 'Golden Ring' saying Mike's name the way it would sound if he had been given the sound of 'L' for the first letter of his name. His name would be 'Like'. Mary would be 'Larry'. We go around until we find someone who has been given this sound to start his first name. Yes, Leslie will be the queen. Her name starts with the letter of the week. Leslie's picture that she has made of herself is put up, and her crown is prepared for the party on Friday.

How important it is to bring *meaningful action* into all learning. Learning that is wrapped in action penetrates our whole body. We move and learn, so every sound has its dance, celebrating its arrival. These letters, which are the picture of the house where the sound lives, become alive for us.

Then the next day, we make a picture of Mother Earth's arms, taking the 'L' into her house. Everything we do is connected to the earth in Kindergarten. At no other time in the child's development is the connection to the earth felt in the marrow of her bones. From her first to fifth years, she is at one with the earth – and every teacher knows this. If an insect comes into the room, or a rainbow is seen in the sky, or thunder calls that the rain is coming, the child is focused on this event as though an inner connection makes them one.

Mother Earth's house is a brown piece of paper with the 'R' and 'L' sides folded to the middle, so that when you open the door or arms of Mother Earth, who is pictured on the inside left, you see the leaf. This large leaf has three pockets. One contains the sun; one the air; one the rain (represented by hints of coloured fluff). This shows that all of these things are part of the leaf: sun, rain, and air.

On the outside stands the upper-case 'L' on the left, and then the lower case 'l' starts on the right. These letters stand under the stars with not a bit of school paste showing. It is by magic that the stars shine, and when the child gets home, the stars on the paper above the letters have been joined by other small stars that have secretly jumped on to the paper. These are small surprises of Kindergarten magic that brings the joy of learning full circle. The teacher is responsible for keeping alive the magic, in whatever form she can manage.

The child now experiences his hands in sand one day, mud the next day, perhaps finger-paint the next day, feeling the form of the letter as he writes it. The richness of the sensory activity that we bring to this moment of forming the letter cannot be overlooked. All this bathing of himself in texture and feeling of the elements connected to the letters must be his before he is asked to throw the lead of the pencil on to the white paper. These dead artefacts as we know them are alive in his mind and body now. They become delightful experiences that glow from the inside out through the dead lead that finds its way on paper.

We then use earth/clay or beeswax to mould the letter. Once we feel good about our creation of the house that holds the sound of 'L', we exchange it for cookie dough. Blessings on all the mothers who have been the Cookie Dough Mother each Wednesday!

We place this dough (what is left of it, for we are just learning to be cooks, and everything must be tasted over and over again) on small silver tins with the poison side turned under.(The shiny side of the foil is poisonous.) It is turned over and the cookie is placed on the dull side. We now place it on the large cookie sheet to bake in our oven. May no Kindergarten room ever be without an oven or a garden. The sand-man brings the cookies to us when we are asleep on our rugs, so that we can dream about 'L' things. All the words we can think of that start with this letter are gathered, sent home, posted, read, and reread.

A Sample Letter to Parents

Dear Parents,

In honour of the historic sounds used in the English language that give wings to our thoughts, the Kindergarten celebrates the Letter of the Week on Friday with a party. Everything we eat at our party will start with that sound. Please see to it that your child has the pleasure of bringing something to the party that we can eat or decorate with on this special occasion.

I am asking you to decorate a shirt or skirt with each week's sound. This has been a source of pleasure in many ways to former Kindergarten children. We will look forward to seeing the picture of the sound appear each week. Some mothers have even made a little picture to go along with the sound.

Never in the life of humanity will the letters that form our speech be as sacred as they are at this moment in the life of the young child. They must go through the same process of early humanity's discovery of being able to feel the holiness of the WORD... and then the slow development that took this sound of WORD, that was a part of his whole body in which everything that was spoken had motion within the life stream of humanity....

The beautiful celebration that took place, of being able to name all that was seen, shook the early humans with joy in the rooting of themselves among all that they claimed as their own.

The hearing and feeling of language was nourishing then to man, as it is now to the young child on the verge of literacy. Our adult language seems somewhat dead today. Words once glowed with aliveness. With a young child we are offered another chance to bring back vitality to this opening up of the language, to again have the opportunity to lay open the vital root system of the genius of language.

The awakening of the written word that began with pictures, and moved slowly through centuries of perfecting the beauty of each symbol as we have it today, is the same as the steps that will be taken in our Kindergarten... for no one cheats oneself of this glory that belongs only to humanity. The dead artifacts that lie on this paper again live within all their life forces when a young child begins the adventure of the written word.

Blessings,

bp

Sound Parties

On Friday, our last day of the week, we eat the things that start with this sound. I remember Marni's mother telling me that she would put her child into the grocery cart and they would go up and down the aisle, filling their cart with everything that started with the sound of the week.

This, the day of Venus, Friday, is our Love Feast – the Sound Party. It is the day for our good manners to shine. It is the Feast of Letters! It is the day we taste over and over again the sound of the week. It is the day we share our gifts of food with our friends. It is the day we can have seconds or thirds for as long as the food lasts. It is the day we are grateful for these gifts the stars have sent to live among us.

We each make a doily. On one side is the letter, both lower case and upper case, surrounded by a border. Then on the other side we draw pictures of everything that starts with that sound. They place the doily on their plates. On the first day the child chooses the plate he wishes – these are placed along the window ledge in order. Here they stand waiting to be used for our cutting and our eating.

The children who have brought food for the Feast of 'L' sit at serving tables with their food in front of them. This food has its own sign celebrating the sound. In the middle of the table sits the gold wooden capital 'L', decorated with all things that sing the word of the letter 'L'.

Then comes the moment when a hush falls over us all. It falls on some of us harder than others. The time of beginning has come. The king or queen rings the 'A' bell and announces that the sound party will begin. The children who have brought the food sit at the table, ready to serve it.

The other children are called up to the Mother's Lap to show the doily placed on their plate where the food will be placed. The teacher writes the lower-case letter on the inside of the left hand and the upper-case on the upper side. Then the child says the sound of 'L' and off they go to use their best manners. 'Please, may I have some?' or 'No, thank you, I haven't learned to like it yet'. We wouldn't want to hurt the feelings of the lettuce who has spent all his days gathering the sun and rain just for this day. We know someday when we have grown to adulthood, we will like it.

I couldn't begin to tell you about all the wonderful food that has been gathered for these 26 letters throughout the years. Once Chipper's mother, feeling the lack of a 'Q' food, made a queen's crown out of a high, round loaf of bread. It was filled with purple violets, surrounded by a cloth of gold; it was a work of art. Not finding enough food for the letter 'Z', she took some small, round rolls and arranged them into the letter 'Z' on the tray. Tim's mother brought red rabbits running in a ring for the 'R' celebration!

When everyone has been served, the chimes ring and seconds may begin. If you want seconds, you go to the child who brought the food you'd like and say, 'Please, may I have another liquorice?'. This goes on until all the food is gone. The children who have brought food feel important and pleased to have so many requests to grant.

And so the week ends with us celebrating the coming of this letter into our lives in written form, wrapped in all the good nurturing of our senses – feeling, touching, tasting, seeing, smelling, loving, and all the others we are discovering that belong to our gateway of learning.

Schedule of Letters

September:	The straight and curved lines, 'l,' 't', and 'r'
October:	o, p, c, g, h
November:	i, th (two weeks), e
December:	d, b (two weeks)
January:	f, w, j, k
February:	f, v, u, ch
March:	ar, f, e
April:	a, sh, g, r
May:	m (two weeks), y, z, x

Yin and Yang

Each letter that we celebrate has its own song, story, poem, singing game, and gesture. This is my version of the story and my song that goes with the letter 'Y':

Yin and Yang

Before the beginning of day – before the earth or the sky, there was Yin and Yang. When Yin was cold, Yang was warm. Warm would look at cold and say, 'I love you so'.

When Yin was wet, Yang was dry. Big would look at small and say, 'I love you so'. When Yin was black, Yang was white, and they would look at each other and say, 'Oh, I love you so'. When Yin was still and Yang was moving, they would look at each other and say, 'I love you so'. When Yin was woman and Yang was man, they would look at each other and say, 'Oh, I love you so'. And as they hugged each other tight, a hard shell grew around them.

Then one day you could hear someone pecking inside it. At last, it cracked open. And there was a dwarf. 'My', he said, as he looked around, 'we need a world'.

Since he was filled with Yin and Yang, he began to make the world. Each day he grew taller and taller. He made high mountains and low mountains.

He made the sky and lifted it high above the earth.

After everything was made, using all the Yin and Yang, he wrote the word 'sun' in the palm of his right hand. He wrote the word 'moon' in the palm of his left hand. He lifted his arms till they touched the high sky. Then he called the word 'sun' seven times. Then he called the word 'moon' seven times. And the moon appeared in the sky. When at last the work of creating the earth and the sky was finished, he lay down and died and his body turned to soil and covered the earth.

(Version by Betty Peck)

We try to follow every story with a song:

Yin Yang opposites, that's how the world began.
(Teacher sings) Well, I am slow.
(Children sing) Well, I am fast.
(Everyone sings) Oh I love your so!
Yin Yang opposites. That's how the world began.

YIN, YANG

Betty Peck

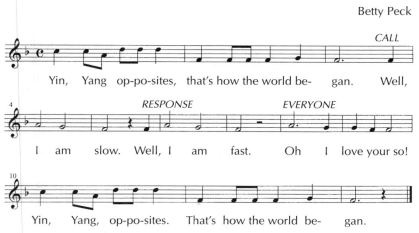

Yin, Yang op-po-sites, that's how the world be- gan. Well, I am slow. Well, I am fast. Oh I love your so! Yin, Yang, op-po-sites. That's how the world be- gan.

Early Numeracy Experience

Finger Numbers

Early man found the number system within his own hands. This is how the Kindergarten child takes the first steps into the mathematical structure of the universe. We start our counting with the little finger of the right hand, and when we reach the fifth finger, which is the thumb, we bend it across our hand and say 'cross over'. This is tallying which we use for all our games and so on, until we have mastered this grouping of fives. When we have mastered the tally system, our next step in the history of man are the finger numbers.

The picture of our finger on paper, sheltered with a roof over its head as he places it on the earth line, gives us a picture of the first number of our next numerical system. These finger numbers, as I call them, become the basis of our study. I am always delighted to say when a child says, 'My father says they are called Roman Numerals', 'Yes, the Romans were the last to use these finger numbers and so some people do call them Roman Numerals'.

As the four fingers separate from the thumb, a 'V' is formed. This is how 'IIIII' was shortened. Ten is also shortened by crossing the arms over each other like an 'X'. We count to ten and then cross our arms saying, 'Crossover' at the same time.

With these finger numbers the child in another way immediately experiences handling the numbers that live within another number. Only finger numbers are used in the Kindergarten until the end of the year. Our experience in writing these numbers day after day makes us long for a new number system that is not so time-consuming. However, the time has been spent with the visual structure of each number.

We have written all the days of November and then December in finger numbers. With the New Year comes the new numbers. But we do not forget that these beautiful finger numbers were one of man's first ways of writing numbers, and that because of this we shall see them everywhere – on old clocks, old buildings, old books, anything of antiquity, for they are loved and sacred to us as part of the cradle of civilization.

And then comes the day when they write how many times the teacher has gone around the Sun on paper. Like the Romans, it will be a long, hard task. To encourage them, I gather hundreds of gold nuggets to give them. Each decade they reach brings them another ten golden nuggets.

Long strips of paper are unrolled as the recording of my years begins. Some children place a golden nugget on each number they have written; some keep them in groups of ten; and some put them in their 'see-through bags'. As soon as they reach my age, they are given another strip on which to draw to show how many times they have gone around the Sun. What a shock it is to them to compare and contrast my age with theirs! They now have 66 golden nuggets to take home, and on that very night I shall see them again at my home to celebrate my birthday.

The New Year brings all things new. And this is the time finger-numbers are replaced by the Hindu Arabic numbers. Each number is introduced in relation to our bodies and the earth line, such as the number one:

> I am one,
> I am the most wonderful
> Under the sun.

We stand with our arms at our sides and stamp our feet to the rhythm. Each number has its own gestures. From now on the recording of numbers takes over. We inventory everything in our Kindergarten room and at home.

My wedding anniversary is on the 3rd of February. I have the children write the ones in the first column, then the tens in the next, and then the tea party numbers... 20 (twen-tea) 30 (thir-tea) in the following column. This year it was 35. When they came to 35, they decorated the number 35. Then they asked Mert how many years she has been married. She said, 'Twenty'. Then they decorated her number. Then they asked Mrs. Rainville, and she says, 'Two'. This number is then decorated. Then they are off flying around, asking all the adults how many years they have been married so they can circle their wedding years on their 'wedding numbers'. All numbers must be meaningful: placing numbers on chairs, calendars, building numbers, numbers on plate, number pages in books, nursery rhymes, books, number pages, family groups, weighing....

Hands

We try to give special care to our hands in the Kindergarten. Our school once provided an exercise teacher, who knew the importance of our bodies' development at this age. The brain needs the hands to be active in order to develop. I feel the need also to provide care for the hands of the children within the classroom.

Many of our poems and singing games are related to using our hands. Whether the children are using crayons, inks, pencils, clay, or finger paint; whether they are sewing, painting, cooking, or cutting, warm-up exercises are needed.

As we prepare to count by tens, we rub each finger first, then stretch them out and in as we count to 100. Then we are ready to write our letters. Before we write our letters, we press the fingers of both hands together and form an 'A'. 'A' is the beginning of our singing sounds. We press our thumbs together and sing A; then index fingers together and sing E; then middle fingers together is I; fourth finger is O; little fingers together U. These are our singing sounds:

A, E, I, O, U

Betty Peck

A, e, i, o, u.   Dear sing-ing sounds how   I   love   you.

Then we dip our fingers into the whisper sounds, such as T, and sing 'Ta, Te, Ti, To, Tu, dear T how I love you'. Sometimes we wear white plastic gloves with the singing sounds written on them for our left hand; at other times we have made puppets for each finger, with 'a, e, i, o, u' written on them. When we hold coloured pencils, we sing our thank-yous to the trees that gave us wood to hold the colour. We snap our thumb, index finger, and middle finger together, singing:

> Thank you, thank you,
> Dear old tree,
> For this gift you give to me.

THANK YOU DEAR OLD TREE

Betty Peck

Thank you, thank you, dear old tree,

For the gift you give to me.

Form Drawing

Drawings were used by early human beings to bring their world down into manageable forms. We find similar designs throughout the world: rhythmical beauty sketched into clay, tooled into wood, printed on textiles. These are human symbols, signs that we have taken the world into ourselves and made it our own.

Each of us must create our own world. We create the world through materials given to us by the gods of: clay, wood, paint, paper, and stone. These materials of the gods must be made available to every child. If we don't provide materials to the children, they will use our walls to write on, as was done in the childhood of civilization when people used the cave walls for their drawings.

I speak with the children about how early men worked to make their drawings perfect. They made their drawings in sand, in the smooth sand of their paths. They wrote them in stone and in wood, until the time came when these designs would be placed on deerskin, on clay pots, woven into rugs, or printed on parchment. The creator touched the material and brought forth life – the life of the ideas, the movements, and all the connections to the universe. The creative soul within humanity vibrated with the cosmos.

Children are put in touch with themselves and their heritage during this experience. These Indian drawings, as they are called in my Kindergarten, also connect them to their surroundings. The mountains, which are a part of our lives in Saratoga, are drawn first and are collected into a book. Before the writing of letters, these straight and curved lines give us the paths to follow in all of our writings; but more than that, they give us the forms to re-create the world as we bring it down onto materials that the gods have provided.

We present the forms we call our alphabet that house the sounds of our mother tongue. There is an orderliness to the presentation. It follows the artistic development of the child which we call language.

Out of the cosmic chaos of the scribble of the child comes the Sun, the circle – which in return becomes the head. Out of this come the trunk and the limbs. Then come the feet; then the feet on the ground. The child comes into her own – this is a truth that is respected.

Then the children are ready to go out to meet the world and see what surrounds them. They experience these ancient forms, capturing these designs that go through their own geometric progression.

Lessons in Form Drawing

Autumn – Big witch hat, little witch hat

Mountains old and new

Indian teepees, near and far away

Spirals

Christmas trees

Three Kings: one from mountains
         one through the woods
         one on the wide seas

Briar Rose

Raindrops on the water

Castle

Colour and Monthly Birthday Boards

When one stands at the Greenwich Observatory in England and sees the stars signalling our next second of life, the feeling of awe is never greater. We stand along with Galileo, the gods and goddesses, and all the lovers of the ancient night-sky drama. These ancient people learned to read the language of the stars. The stars told them when to plant and when winter would turn to spring. It is here in the sky above us that our calendar is written. And to show our gratefulness we always record their life's work here in our Kindergarten room. Their gift of the calendar that we now use is stretched out from the beginning of the year to the end. And what's more, these small pieces of paper that hold our days have the dates of our births along with all the other events that fill the year.

Almost everyone we have ever heard of has a place on our birthday boards. They are written, not just for writing-down's sake, but so that we can feel a part of this connection with the celebration of life and be truly thankful for it.

As we know, the calendar is written in the sky. In our Kindergarten you learn that everything in the universe is brought down on paper. All that has gone into this process of translating it on to paper is a lifetime study in itself. I have chosen with great care the colour that I feel represents each moon month. What does the full moon see as it looks down over our land? The moon sees a beautiful colour cloth wrapped around each birthday board according to its seasonal colours.

The Kindergarten's favourite colour is red, and its favourite month is **December**. The colour on the birthday board for December is red. This is the month chosen by the Christians for the Christmas Baby, and for Father Christmas, who wears a red velvet robe in our Kindergarten. It is also my birthday month – I find red to be life-giving. So red becomes the colour for the December birthday board.

January's birthday board is white. Virgin white... the New Year... the white of the long beard of the old year's Father Time... the face of Janus looking backward and forward... the coming of the New Year as a babe wrapped in white for purity... the beginning... the permission to begin again... the celebration of white snow that comes to our mountain tops... the fragile snowflakes that in their six-ness are so like us and yet so different.... That's why we love them so. Each snowflake is as different as we are different. We have now filled six years with our living, and even the rest of us are in their sixth year.

Outside our schoolroom door, the white snowbells are in bloom. How important it is to have a story for everything that grows in our garden. The story of the snowbell goes somewhat like this:

The colours were given out in summer. 'Oh, I do hope I get red'. said the tomato. 'Of course, you shall have red', said the Giver of All Colours.

'I do want orange', said the pumpkin. 'Yes, you may have orange.' And so the pumpkin became orange.

'I do hope I can have yellow for my colour', said the lemon. And so the lemon was given yellow.

'Oh', said the grass, 'I want green'. And the Giver of All Colours said, 'Yes, you may have green'.

Both sky *and* lake wanted blue. 'If I get blue', said sky, 'I shall give a bit of my colour to all of the great families of water.' And blue was indeed given to sky, who shone her blue down on all the great bodies of water.

And the cornflower said, 'I wish I could also be blue'. The Giver of All Colours said, 'Don't be sad. I have a very special dark blue for you. It's called indigo.'

Then iris said, 'Please may I have purple?'. 'Of course, you may, dear Iris....'

Well, it was a glorious summer. Everyone dressed in his own beautiful colour. But when winter came, no one had thought of snow, so snow had to go through the world looking for just the right colour. It asked the iris for its purple. It asked the cornflower for its indigo. It asked the sky for its blue. It asked the grass for its green. It asked the lemon for its yellow. It asked the pumpkin for its orange. It asked the tomato for its red. No one was willing to give snow their colour.

One day snow saw a little white flower dancing in the wind. 'May I have some of your white?' 'Yes, you may', said the little flower. 'Here, take white from me.' And if you look very carefully at the flower's petals, you can see where part of the white has been taken off.

'Because you were so kind to give me your colour', said the snow, 'you shall be the very first flower to come up through my snow each year and you shall be called Snowbell.'

Author unknown

On New Year's Day, the guests who come to my house draw pictures of Janus, the Roman god whose name brings the word January. This god's head faces both ways at once. These pictures that the guests have drawn are put on swords after we do the Morris Dance, a sword dance forming the star of David. We carry the sword banners through the house singing, 'Here we come a-wassailing', until we come to the feast table. There on the table is the New Year's gift. The year that is ending is recorded with pictures, letters, pressed flowers, news clippings, and cards for every occasion. After they have been pasted in, the book of the year is closed on the day the new book is presented... to again record the family's events. These New Year books are to be kept and enjoyed for ever.

Grey is the colour of our birthday boards that I've chosen for **February**. February's grey days in winter set the stage for spring to come. These grey days are made glad by the heart of Saint Valentine. By this time all the white dress-ups in the Kindergarten have turned grey. Mothers look at the basket of white dress-ups and plead to take them home to wash, but they do not go home until after the greyness of February.

March and spring-green need no explanation. The world in Saratoga is this colour of new life. Each new leaf is singing its song in spring-green.

The colour for **April** is pink. It was when my daughter was five that the birthday boards were first made. It was her birthday month, and her favourite colour was pink. In fact, at five years old she longed to name her children Pink Icing and Red Lipstick.

My cousin Kathy and I sat and thought how best to make these boards to show the whole year. We decided to cover the boards with corduroy. The boards were about 12 by 18 inches in size, like wall calendars. We marked out all the days of the month with horizontal and vertical strings of yarn for these wall calendars. We hung folded papers over the yarn strips for each day's number.

As the year rolls by, every ounce of work in preparing these boards becomes worth it when you see the learning that takes place through them. I always enjoy the first day, when the children arrive in the Kindergarten room with their mothers and the birthday boards come alive as each child places her name on the day of her birth.

The birthday boards give us a visual picture of the whole year, stretched out before us. They nurture the sense of anticipation, so important for the human spirit. Anticipation strengthens the sense of hope, as well as our arithmetical concepts.

These squares of coloured paper matching the colour of the boards are a far cry from the celestial heavens from which our calendar comes. In ancient times, the dramatic charting of the magnificent planets, stars, and celestial bodies that give life to our small world was set down. We display this gift that has been handed down to us and call it our birthday boards.

The colour for **May** is yellow. This yellow is not the gold of the fall, but a soft yellow that indeed matches the sunshine. Yellow and green ribbons decorate the Maypole on the first day of May.

I choose the colours that are the most meaningful in all ways for the month. In May, yellow roses and yellow marguerites flood our room. We also have yellow curtains that match our floor here in the Kindergarten room. Spring-born children feel the spring colours of spring-green, pink, and yellow as their own. Summer-born children feel the blues and purples as their own.

The colour for **June** is blue, a light blue. Blue is for the water of the lakes, the rivers, and our swimming pools. It is this month that calls us out to the 'wild blue yonder'. The colour for **July** is dark blue, indigo, the blue of the flag – the red, white, and blue.

The colour for **August**, the kingly month, is purple. Purple is the last of the rainbow colours, and in August we have the last days of summer, before we nestle in again on our return to school.

It is important for me to feel my roots in the Kindergarten room... my meaning, my love of beauty, my healing in every corner of the room. Then life-giving qualities flow into me. In this way I am enriched to give and give and give. This is why the colours are chosen, to give just the right enriched feelings.

The colour for the **September** birthday board is brown. In the autumn we sit around our indoor garden and look into the brown birthday calendar. This is the first time we experience the birthday boards, these little squares that house the day. Of course, knowing that the calendar is written in the sky, we bring it down to earth as a gift we owe to all those who spent their lives looking at the night sky, watching and recording century after century, in order to give us these little squares we look at that are our numbered days.

I chose brown for September because the child hides or encloses himself in the welcoming arms of school – awakening into the new authority, finding new friends… new adventures, new awe, new joys for a few hours each week. I chose brown for September because it is Mother Earth's colour. She starts now to call her children back to her brown earth.

I feel good about flooding the room with browns of every hue to welcome the new Kindergarten children. It is how starting seems – death into life. It is my connecting colour for the room where one meets new life. The preparation of the brown soil for these seeds is the welcome I give. The Kindergarten room has all the qualities of an enriched, comfortable, artistic dwelling that invites families to place their treasures into the hands of the gardener, who is humbled by this trust.

The heat of summer days mixes with the gold of autumn, making orange pumpkins. This pumpkin colour is the colour of the **October** birthday board. Each year in the spring we have our ceremony of planting the pumpkin seeds (everything in the Kindergarten is a ceremony). It is these pumpkins that we now open in October. We divide the treasures from Mother Earth's treasure houses into three – some to eat, some to save for planting, and some to give as gifts.

In Kindergarten we try to do everything in threes. It gives the child the feeling of structure that is the fibre of all the universe – the family unit, the cosmic connection, the stability of form, the trinity, the body, soul, and spirit. We bring out these pumpkin seeds, filled with the memories of autumn, when the room was covered with orange, the colour we discovered hiding in red and yellow.

There are many ways to have children experience this discovery of orange. One of the most effective ways I have discovered is to stretch white paper across the floor. The children sit crossed-legged along the edge of the paper. The teacher says, 'This is the best I could do in giving you the earth. Since I couldn't bring the earth to give you, all I have is this white paper. Can you pretend to see how brown it is with all the soil, all the leaves, all the butterfly wings?… Here comes the rain on this old earth.'

I use prepared starch that looks blue. The finger painting begins. The children feel its wetness, and by this time are into the game. Then I say, 'Oh, I wish I could give you the sun, for all the earth needs sun. But how can I do it?' Of course someone says, 'With yellow paint!'

'Yes', I say. There are never enough 'yeses' for the five-year-old. My friend Margret Meyerkort says 'yes' even though nothing is going on; just a beautiful, shimmering 'yes' springs forth from her lips. I'm sure she feels it as all of us do that there are not enough 'yeses' in the world, especially for the child of this age. I say 'yes' with everything: 'Yes, you may, but not now. We are busy doing this job. Don't forget, it will be your turn later.... Yes, you may.' 'Yeses' are beautiful words to hear.

So yes, I take my yellow paint from the jar and put a bit of sunshine into everyone's rain. These are the two great needed opposites in everyone's life. The children delight in making great, glorious circles of sunshine.

Then as a surprise I come with the hottest part of the sun, the red-hot fire, by saying, 'Oh, so you think I forgot that the sun has a heart of fire. The very hottest part of the sun is coming now. It is like your heart and my heart. I am very much like the sun and very different from the sun. That is why I love the sun so much.' (This is said throughout the day in everything we see: I am very much like the _____ and very different.)

'I would not forget the heart of the sun.' And by now they are shouting 'Red!'. Yes, it is red! I put the red in the middle of their yellow. And then I turn to see them now with both hands making two large circles bumping into each other. But now it is orange I see. 'Orange!', I say. 'I didn't give you orange. Yes, where did you get the orange?' Then they scream, 'Red and yellow together!' 'Do you mean to say that orange was hiding inside those two colours? Was it hiding inside red and yellow?' 'Yes!' By now both their hands are going in circles in the yellow paint and red paint. And before them now sits a pumpkin. Will they see it as pure pleasure in the colour, or as pumpkin pie, or as Cinderella's coach, or as Mother Earth's Treasure House, or as another step in their creation of the world?

It is important for the teacher to know when to find the stopping place. It is equally important for her to plan the steps that follow every activity. Now off they go outside to wash their hands in the great 'silver sea', the stainless-steel bowl full of warm water. They soon turn the water into 'orange juice' as they wash their hands in pure delight of colour.

At this time the sound of the week is the letter 'P', of course, and our shoulders are the earth and our heads are the pumpkins, whose roots go down below the earth for the lower-case letter 'p'.

During the month of October we also have the letter 'C', found in the curve of our left arm. We can take our right hand, start at our fingertips, and follow the path to our heart, saying, 'Come to my heart. Come to my heart and see'. The children love to find C's with bending their fingers. It is delightful to see the children curling their whole bodies up like C's.

In our garden we grow calendulas. We harvest the seeds of the calendula plant, 'Mary's gold', and find that they are in the shape of the letter 'C'. Now we have more orange colour from the petals of the calendula for our salads, soups, and vases. We take our honey crayons and make the pumpkin out of two C's. We draw two C's on either side, turned toward the middle, to form the pumpkin growing in the field.

And so this colour orange fills our life in autumn. It is here that I present the story of the umbilical cord wrapped in the truth of imagination. Never is a pumpkin allowed in the room without its silver cord. When we go out, finding our pumpkin in the Welches' garden in years when our own Kindergarten crop has been unsuccessful, we are careful to bring the connecting stem, along with the roots and all, back with the pumpkin. The Kindergarten extended family reaches out to the neighbourhood and beyond. The Welches always plant extra ones for us just in case we need them.

After the pumpkin is properly placed in our indoor garden during the month of October, I stand with my hand placed over my own print of my silver cord and say, 'Everyone has their silver cord. Every fruit, every bug, every lamb, every squirrel has its own silver cord'.

Then the magnolia tree that was planted for Dale, who was a part of my Kindergarten family before he died, gives up its treasure houses: seed pods filled with red seeds. I gather them each year as I think of that dear little boy who is five years old forever, and of his picture that he helped his mother paint of the first schoolhouse here in Saratoga. It was always a part of our Kindergarten room decor. I bring the magnolia pods from this tree into the classroom, and each child is delighted to see the beautiful silver cord of each seed being pulled out as it leaves the nest. We say together, 'Goodbye, Mother, goodbye', as the seed, this treasure, leaves the mother and goes out into the world. Soon every child notices silver cords everywhere – in the apple, in the tomato, on the grapevine....

One day the silver cord breaks off the pumpkin and we see only the print of this vital connection. We know the pumpkin is very much like us but also very different; that's why we love it so. We put our hands over the print left by our own silver cord when we were born. Yes, we have all lost our own silver cord.

Over and over again, we connect ourselves to the earth in all ways. We are akin to something larger than ourselves, being part of this giant 'whole'. Feeling this, we become responsible and grateful, as though we have a special calling to protect the earth as she provides for us.

Along the row of birthday boards the next fall colour is gold. Gold is for **November**.

> It's the golden in the garden,
> It's the golden in the glen.
> It's golden, golden, golden,
> November is here again!

Everything in our Kindergarten garden is gold: leaves from the black walnut tree, wisteria leaves that spread out into the sycamore trees that are over our heads when we go out of our Kindergarten door.... 'Now is November, the time to remember to say thank you.' This is a saying from Margaret White given long ago when my children were in Kindergarten.

It was in the autumn of the year that the finishing touches on the new Kindergarten room were made. I had been asked by the Principal to be the Kindergarten teacher at his school.

There had not been a Kindergarten at this school for many years. The architect asked me to come and choose the material for the floor. Well, of course, I already knew what I wanted – hardwood floors. It never dawned on me that the importance of such a request could be questioned. No, it could not be wood. I was shown two pieces of floor tile – one, a scratchy beige and the other, yellow-gold. They were both out of the question. Then I said, 'Let's just keep this floor we have now [it was a plywood sub-floor] and stain and polish it, so that we can see and feel the grain's exquisite pattern'. At that moment I looked up and, through our windows that were across the eastern side of the room, I saw the leaves of the catalpa tree brushing against the windows that went from our low shelf to the ceiling. These leaves were the same colour as the yellow-gold floor tile.

The Kindergarten world calls out for beauty. To stand on hardwood floors is a must for the Kindergarten child. Where are the architects who stand for beauty in our school buildings?

The catalpa tree looks down on our gold floor from outside our window and redeems the situation, once each year in September, when the tree and the room are one.

THE CATALPA TREE

The catalpa leaves are matching the floor,
Matching the floor, matching the floor,
With their bright yellow-gold paint.

The catalpa leaves are falling on me, falling on me,
The catalpa leaves are falling on me,
Have you ever been kissed by a leaf?

The catalpa leaves are rustling below, rustling below,
The catalpa leaves are rustling below,
With the help of five-year-old feet.

The catalpa leaves are flying away, flying away, flying away,
The catalpa leaves are flying away,
On their way to becoming something new.

                            bp

At this time of year in November, the flowers in our garden are again yellow and gold. The whole room decor is trimmed with yellows and gold. I wear dresses with this colour, and the paper we use for our books is gold. We bathe in this colour through all of our senses. And so we have the year's cycle stretched out to see, to compare, to contrast, to feel, and to count.

Drama

At the end of the week we dramatize the story that we have listened to and illustrated all week long. Of course, it is not hard for the teacher to tell what character each child wishes to be, as they have been talking about their roles since the first day that they heard the story. 'You will be chosen' is my way of saying that I will choose the characters. I want them to experience the feeling of being chosen, of being the special one.

Often I ask the children what parts are needed in the play. They may say, 'We need rocks', or 'We need the water'. I write their ideas down on a large sheet of paper that I have put up on the wall. Seeing the importance of the listing of the 'cast' gives them a form of order that structures the preparation. This procedure is part of the play process... the drama world. It is the teacher's role to link the children to the culture of both past and present. In so doing, certain patterns of limits are set in order to prepare for the future.

There is a form in which one begins this step into the world of drama. One of the ways we get into this form in Kindergarten is by making a list of characters. Later we decide where the audience will sit. We choose the costumes, and we learn to take our bows.... All these things are part of our culture of presenting dramas. The teacher must always seek to link the child with the culture, helping him to see where he fits in, and making him feel comfortable there. In the child's daily play, she herself is trying on the culture all the time, playing out her role and trying to see where she fits.

I have learned to choose the important character first. I say, 'Would you like to be the princess, Heather?', looking at the one who has most wanted to be the princess all week. If I ask first who wants to be the tree, no one will answer because everyone is waiting to choose the role of the princess or the king. Afterwards, others are free to choose and create the roles they want – they delight in being the rocks, water, trees. Shiro was the youngest boy in the class: he was chosen to be the tallest tree in the forest. Now each time we had a play, he wished to be the tallest tree in the forest.

When everyone has been chosen, they find the dress-up that will be best for them. As they wrap themselves up in great comfort and security, they sense exactly what a tree looks like, exactly how a witch is dressed, or exactly how the water should look. They tie, pin, and knot the material together, perhaps adding a crown on top of everything. (Crowns are worn throughout the day.) For a child to feel like a kingly tree is important.

Several years ago when I was in England at Henry Pluckrose's school, Prior Weston, I watched the preparations for a pageant the school was going to give. Margo, the main music teacher, was listening to one of the children. The child had been chosen to be a pirate and was saying, 'I don't have a costume to wear'. 'Oh', she said, 'it's just a "dressing up". You don't have to have a costume. It's just a dressing up.' I remember seeing how relieved the child was when he knew he would be free to choose to wear whatever he thought that a pirate should wear. And so in my California Kindergarten, we call our basket of veils and materials, the 'dress-ups'.

When all preparations are done, there is something known as the 'readiness hush' that falls on everyone as he stands in his place. The players are then introduced, and in response to the introduction, they bow to the audience. Of course, the audience is sometimes just a chair where the bear sits, but nevertheless, they know the direction in which to face when they bow.

This format of introducing the characters was the suggestion of a child to improve the play that we had done one particular week. We tried the introduction of characters, and it proved such a success that it has always been part of our presentations ever since. Each child is named and her part in the play is told. The announcer is always announced last. The announcer holds a beautiful Montessori bell that rings throughout our Kindergarten room and the world, to announce the beginning of the play. Circles of sound radiate out from the bell, continuing out to the cosmos. When we can no longer hear them, the announcer announces the name of the play. The room is silent; we all feel the anticipation of the moment. I start the story with 'Once upon a time', walking them through their parts. This makes it possible for everyone to feel as though they can bring their part to life. I tell the story, and they fill in the words when they are able.

Some classes hardly need my words at all; on some occasions they even take my place. For some I am walking through the story with their hand in mine, though I step back when I feel their wings take flight. Having heard the story over and over, together we bring the story to life, the children making it their own.

You can feel them entering into each other's parts, and I often hear more than one child saying the words. Because I am there with them when it comes to their turn, they know, having watched at other times, that they will do well. Never is it time lost, but time gained, when they see you helping someone on any level, for they know help is there for them when they need it. Everyone feels the importance of his part, even the roles of the water, the snow, the rainbow. What are children telling us when they delight in being inanimate objects? Do they hear the whispers from these objects that we so take for granted?

At the end of the play, the announcer rings the bell again, announcing the end of the play. At that time, we all curtsy or bow. Then it is clean up time. Everything is restored to order and beauty. How wonderful to have this habit of making way for the new. It is a vital part of the production, and everyone feels their responsibility for cleaning the room. The words of the song 'Who will help? Who will help? Who will help, says the little red hen' bring the play to its completion.

WHO WILL HELP?

Betty Peck

'Who will help?'　'Who will help?'　'Who will help?' said the lit-tle red hen.

I have learned over the years never to have the play on the Friday before any holiday. There are so many levels to explore on any holiday. You work to arrange everything for the celebration, which is usually a play. Then it is nice to enjoy this setting and use it in as many ways as you can the next day – the room is at its best, so keep it awhile. You can use the same setting leisurely to evaluate the event with the children the next day, by which process new standards can be set up. We refer to them with the children's names: 'Let's do Taliesin's idea and have everyone bow as we say their names.' 'Let's ring bells to tell the story has begun', says Chipper. Then we add to this idea by saying, 'And what shall we do to end the play?' 'Well', says Chipper, 'we can still ring the bells'.

Out of this discussion comes the format for our plays. Each child feels related to the drama because it has become a part of himself... talking it over, enjoying, and savoring those moments that we all shared. This child has wrapped the wisdom of the story deep inside his heart, to be unwrapped and used many times through his life.

Animals in the Classroom

Caring for those more helpless than you is always a part of life itself and it certainly is a part of every classroom. It is important to be a part of the life cycle of any creature that is found in the garden. I raise butterflies for the garden, and this event was always the cause of much celebration and poster-making. This can be done throughout the autumn and spring. Silkworms and mulberry trees were always a part of our lives in many ways.

At Easter we hatch chickens, with our hatchery giving them to us ready to hatch on any day we specify. I feel that waiting for 21 days is too much for Kindergarten children to comprehend. Sometimes we are lucky enough to have a hen hatch her eggs in our Kindergarten. With this important event of a chick hatching without the mother hen, we take the first to hatch and set this new life in the middle of our golden ring. With the children we think of all the ways the chick is like us and all the ways this fluff of new life is different. We sing the sameness and differences with our song, Yin Yang, which ends '...that's why I love you so'. If you hatch chickens in the classroom, it is important to find a family like Nadara's family who will take the chicks to bond with their mother hen.

Our bears hibernate all winter long. We build a cave in the room, and the children may go in to visit Bear, but Bear does not come out until Spring. At that time, Mother Bear and Baby Bear, who has been born in winter, come out together – this always demands a celebration. We were invited once in February to bring our Teddy bears and come to the library for a bear party. When I said, 'No, our bears are hibernating and will not be out till Spring', the librarian was shocked. It is one of the jobs of the Kindergarten teacher to educate the faculty and administration.

For years, I brought my collie, Chelsea, with me as part of the Kindergarten. The children all loved her. She loved her days with us so much that she even went down to school on Saturday and Sundays and waited there for school to start. She never did learn the days of the week before she died.

My assistant, Jenni, then brought her dog for seven years. We all loved Boozer. When Jenni was first chosen to be my assistant, she wanted to know if she should change the dog's name. I said, 'no.' He was a black Labrador who often had to be retrained in front of all of our eyes. It was always a spectacular lesson for all of us to watch Jenni retrain her dog. The children would often say of someone who had forgotten how wonderful they were that perhaps they needed to be retrained.

The garden supplies many insects and snails. At one time, we had a snail service. During the week we would gather the snails in special buckets from our garden and leave them by the garden gate. On Friday the snails would be picked up by a company that specialized in 'escargot'. They were delighted to have these snails because we did not use poison in our garden.

We always had plenty of earthworms and birds that needed to be fed. The children brought in rabbit droppings for earthworms and bread crumbs for the birds. The bird-bath was kept full of water for the birds. Our activities include a visit to the dairy, where Mr. Peake had his cows, pigs, and chickens for us to see. During the last two weeks of school, we have homing pigeons in the room, which fly home with great ceremony on the last day of school.

There have been years when we would have dog day and cat day. On these days, by appointment, we would have the family pet visit our class. We would have our dog book ready on dog day to draw the pictures of the dog and record his visit. We would do the same for cats.

At one time we had ducks until, to their horror, the janitors would find them swimming in the toilets. At one time I even had a bird aviary in the middle of the room. However, I feel that with a garden outside our Kindergarten door, I find the children's relationships with each other far outweigh the need always to have animals in the room.

Discoveries

For many years, I would keep a Discovery Book in the classroom. Each discovery made by the teacher or a child was written in the Discovery Book. The child making the discovery was therefore in charge of each similar situation that would arise. Here are some Discovery Book vignettes illustrating just some of the discoveries made by the Kindergarten children.

1973

DAVID discovered he could ask the teacher for help.
David discovered how to climb the redwood tree.
David discovered even numbers. Other numbers are uneven.
David discovered that sadness can come if you're counting on something and it doesn't happen.
David discovered that he needed a place to sit that was his own. So, when he had to leave, he could always count on a special place to come back to.
David discovered that if you say something untruthful about a person's work, they might believe it's true, so you must rush to them and tell of the mistake so their feelings will be protected.
David discovered that if someone spoils your drawing you can forgive them, and turn your paper over to a new side.

JANET discovered that if you write with the blue pencil on a wet surface, it is darker than if you write on the dry surface.
Janet discovered that two squares make a rectangle.
Janet discovered that you can use the other side of the rake to smooth.
Janet discovered that books take the sadness away and make you feel better.

CHRIS discovered private property.
Chris discovered care of equipment. Equipment hasn't anyone else to look after it and take care of it, but you and me.
Chris discovered that if you didn't know how to pull the paper off the roll, you would waste so much... therefore, you need to have a lesson.

Chris discovered that if some things are high and hard to reach, they are not meant for him to use.

Chris discovered in January that it feels wonderful to be helpful and everybody feels proud of you for being helpful, especially the teacher.

Chris discovered the first ladybug in our garden.

Chris discovered that our pumpkin was trying to return to the earth from the inside.

SANDRA discovered it is important to sit where you can see.

Sandra discovered it is heavier with three people than with two.

Sandra discovered that her baby-sitter was not home, so she decided to come back to school to be safe.

Sandra discovered that Sylvia can be queen on 'S' day.

Sandra discovered that when everyone talks at the same time, noise fills the air and she does not like it.

Sandra discovered that if you can't reach, you can pass it along.

Sandra discovered that if you sit in the sun, she can't see.

ALEX discovered an unread page. We had all missed the last page.

Alex discovered the shelves in the storybook house were made for different sized books: large books on the top shelf, small books on the lowest shelf.

Alex discovered that two boys cannot stand on one chair. One is certain to fall off.

Alex discovered that you could wash pumpkin seeds that were returning to the earth and dry them to prepare for planting.

LISA discovered that you only use as many pages in your book as you are years old: 5 years, 5 pages; 6 years, 6 pages.

Lisa discovered that if the rings are slippery, you will fall off.

Lisa discovered that if you write smaller you will have room to write larger words.

Lisa discovered that people need to know honest problems and not ones made up to trick people. Her trick could have put other people into trouble.

STEVEN discovered that you only push people when they ask you to... otherwise, your job is to be there to help them....

Steven discovered that if you say 'no', you do not like the story when you really did, it makes everyone feel sad.

Steven discovered that indoor equipment stays indoors.

Steven discovered he gets hungry, so he ate the best of everything he could find and he discovered that friends did not like this.

Steven discovered that if he asked for food, he could have some.

Steven discovered that people do not want to sit next to you if they think you're mean.

Steven discovered that there is plenty of room for a target, and that they are fun to make.

Steven discovered how to flip under the redwood tree.

Steven discovered three shovels under the structure.

STACEY discovered how people take turns. If no one is waiting, your turn may go on forever. If someone is waiting to have a turn, then you must feel when it is best to stop.

Stacey discovered that you must return things to their special place so they won't get lost.

Stacey discovered that noise hurts your ears... and pollutes the air.

Stacey discovered that if you bother someone who is listening she won't be able to hear.

Stacey discovered that if everyone helps we can get the job done faster.

Stacey discovered that you can blow bubbles with soap.

MRS PECK: I discovered that purple paint stains the floor.

I discovered that upstairs in the playhouse is a good secret place for the blocks.

I discovered a wonderful art gallery outside our room in the hall.

I discovered we must make gift envelopes. Otherwise, we need to use more tape than we have, and the tape hides our beautiful pictures.

I discovered that if you sit on the train and push it with your feet, there is a lovely squeak sound which I like. I do not like the thunder sound when I am trying to help someone. But I really love real thunder.

I discovered on Valentine's day heart-shaped leaves on the sweet potato shouting 'Happy Valentine's Day' in green.

PART VI

The Kindergarten Teacher

The Kindergarten Teacher 'On Stage'

My Kindergarten teaching is 99 per cent preparation. Before I get out of bed, I take the early-morning time to plan the Kindergarten day. In the quietness of dawn, before the day has started, ideas flow to me, always too many for one day. When I have thought them through and put them into order, I know the children will also intuit with me the evolutionary process of the day.

As a Kindergarten teacher, I find myself being an actress, and also a director and a stage manager. I set the stage for the day's activities. Each morning is different, yet fundamentally the same. I want my room ordered 'to the bone' and every action planned, like a script, ready on the tip of my tongue. I need to be able to put my hand on anything in the room, to know where everything is at all times. I have paper cut to size in the chosen colour, and the necessary equipment to carry out each idea. Continuous, well-planned, powerful structure and scenarios are the underpinnings to support the flow of both the children's creativity and of mine to flow throughout the day, wrapped around the needs that are brought through the door by each child welcoming the surprise demands of the day.

Dress

My Kindergarten clothes are truly my secret costumes. With my whole being I am saying, 'I love life', and 'I love being a Kindergarten teacher'. My wardrobe mistresses are the designers in town, the local 'Goodwill Industries', and friends who find just the dress they know I will need and love for different occasions. Sometimes I have my clothes designed so that I feel free to sit on the floor with the children, and catch or even hide them in the folds of my skirts. When the children dress up in the Kindergarten, I, too, know the magic that comes with dressing up.

In my beginning years as a teacher I wore a German dirndl as my teaching outfit. One day the principal of the American school where I was teaching asked me: 'Why do you dress this way? Other teachers are commenting.' I explained that Froebel, who was German, had given to the world the word 'Kindergarten', and I wanted to wear the German national dress in his honour as well as for the country that holds such fairy-tale folklore. With the dirndl I wore Italian shoes, which represented Maria Montessori's influence on my life. My blouses were inherited from the long line of teachers in my husband's family. I often wore a beautiful long gold chain and watch that had belonged to my husband's mother, a creative-writing teacher for 27 years. No one questioned my Kindergarten clothes again, although I am sure my colleagues were occasionally amazed at the combinations I chose. I wore the German dirndl for years until my waistline changed. I found a designer who knew how to put together beautiful Afghan walking dresses, which are a part of my wardrobe to this day.

I myself have two large trunks full of inspiring garments. In one are costumes kept from Dorothea Johnston's days in the theatre, bequeathed to me from her travels abroad when she spread the beauty of the North American Indian culture through stories, songs, and dances. In the other trunk are costumes she wore when she produced 'A Midsummer Night's Dream' and other Shakespearean plays. One day I saw a clothes-line full of astoundingly beautiful clothes dripping in the children's play garden. Where did these clothes come from, I asked? 'Oh', said Louise Easterbrook, from whom we rented the farm, 'the neighbour up the street buys all her clothes in Paris. She was getting rid of some of them and I told her the children would love them for dress-up clothes.' I gathered them up, took them home, and wore them myself with gratitude for years.

A poet once said: 'I think fashion shows the inadequacy of God, for God knew how to clothe each creature of the earth. He had no problem with design and colour of the butterfly, or any of the insects or animals or the fish of the sea, but when it came to human beings, He did not know what to choose. So when we dress ourselves in beauty, we, too, become as the gods'.

As a Kindergarten teacher, I choose the natural fibres of pure cotton, wool, and silk, for I like to express out loud my gratitude to the giver of these materials in the dress of the children as well as myself. I believe that every child deserves to experience the most beautiful colours and materials. 'I see you are wearing cotton from the cotton plant today', I say. On the many occasions when I needed to change a child's attention, such as when recovering from a fall, I might say: 'Did you see the sheep that gave you her wool? I wonder where she lives?' Or 'Your silk cape looks as if there are ten million fairies dancing in it. Thank you, dear silkworm, for your gift to me. Thank you to the princess who first saw the sparkling thread you spun and wanted to weave more together so that she would walk in beauty wearing your gift.'

Whenever I go walking with the Kindergarten children or when we work in the garden on warm sunny days, I always wear a hat. I keep a wide-brimmed garden hat near the door that leads out to the garden, during the rest of the year. You see it there with the tools as you enter the Kindergarten. Comfortable shoes are also part of my 'armour'. I often find quaint ones in antique stores with tie-up laces and unusual designs. When I return to my home, I shed the day by exchanging my Kindergarten clothes for what brings me back to the bosom of my family. I have inherited a good many beautiful clothes from my husband's family. His father was born in China, so I have many robes that hang on my doors and walls as art pieces. I throw them over my garden clothes when I entertain.

I feel that the wise old women found in many fairy tales could not have gathered better wardrobes than the ones I've gathered over the years. If a teacher looks at her best, she can forget herself and plunge into the activity of the day dressed in comfortable beauty. This ignites her spirits and can light the way for everyone. Setting the tone for the day can be done simply by wearing colour and design in her dress. For each season in the Kindergarten I choose colours nourishing for the children and myself. In autumn – September and October – I wear gold, orange, brown, and ochre to match the leaves that are returning to Mother Earth. I choose jewellery that has leaves and tendrils as part of the design – handmade necklaces and bracelets that tell a story. I often wear flowers in my hair – I always wear something in my hair from the garden.

In November the flowers in our Kindergarten garden again are yellow and gold. The whole room is trimmed with yellows and golds, and I wear dresses with these colours. With the paper we use for our writing books of yellow and golden hue, we bathe in this part of the rainbow spectrum.

As Christmas approaches, I extend myself to match the season in its feeling of anticipation and good will. My clothes radiate with reds and greens and purples. They are printed with roses and stars, and filled with sparkles. I wear long chains of bells or stars around my neck. In ancient civilizations, the dye for the colour purple came from a shellfish found in the Mediterranean Sea. Since each shellfish yielded only a small quantity of dye, the colour was expensive. Because of its high cost and its ennobling sobriety, purple became the symbol of rulers.

In winter I purposefully wear shades of black and grey, filled with white picturesque patterns of snow, red hearts, and other appropriate designs. The black and grey colour serve as a springboard for the sunny yellows, pinks, and spring green that I wear to celebrate Spring. The catalpa tree outside our window is delicately budding in spring green, lifting our spirits in knowing we are all one with nature. Pastel pinks and apricot colours give a gentle glow for five-year-olds to gather strength for their own growing.

At Easter I wear lavender and place touches of purple everywhere in the room, and only on Mother's Day and when the birds fly do I wear blue. The old masters always clothed their Madonna figures in this colour. I wear a blue dress to celebrate mothers everywhere.

Again in June I wear the colours of the sea and skies – the blues of the Bluebird of Happiness. When 'the birds fly' – my expression for the last day of school – I want to be part of that picture with my matching blue. My jewellery of butterflies and birds is saved for this time of year.

Teacher's Throne

For many years I have referred to the special place where our Kindergarten teachers sit as 'The Teacher's Throne'. A place of beauty built by parents, it is here she gathers the children around her for stories of the garden, celebrations, singing, and peaceful activities. This special place honours the teacher. It often becomes the centre of play in the garden, more so than a place for the teacher to sit. It gives the children a place to play teacher, house, office, school.

Picturesque Speech from the Kindergarten Teacher

Kindergarten children need to hear their relationship to you, the earth, and themselves, released from limiting factual communication and expanded into imaginative pictures of living form. This, in turn, gives them permission to feel their own creative energies as an aspect of the solution to the challenge of 'making life work'. Children enter the world vitally connected to the aliveness in all they see, feel, touch, and hear. The Kindergarten teacher will enrich this relationship to the child's world if she uses picturesque speech. Here are some of the examples I use:

'Your jacket is crying on the floor': This phrase not only told how the jacket felt being without a home, but gave the child a chance to use compassion, at the same time deepening his sense of order.

'We do not hurt people on the outside or the inside': The Kindergarten child already had experienced hurt feelings, but to have it linked with outside bodily wounds helped emphasize the need to protect each other.

'The bees were having parties with the flowers': Sex education can take many forms. The need for each other can be established as well as the give-and-take of life.

'It's moon-boat time': This song called the children to come and sit in a semicircle where half the class was gathered to hear the teacher as she told the story. As every teacher knows, there is a strong relationship

to the moon, especially the full moon. The shape of the crescent moon is peaceful. When they see it in the sky, they can see the place assigned to them, making them feel more at home in the great cosmos.

'This is the day the birds will fly': Never were the words 'the last day of school' spoken. Learning and going to school should never end. The children felt like birds getting ready to fly. Even the teacher herself felt this restlessness in the air.

'Did you hear the bell calling your name?': Each child brought a bell from home that could call his name when the teacher rang it. These bells were sewn onto something special, such as a knitted scarecrow doll, kept near the door of the classroom.

'The letters are a gift from the stars': All letters are written from the top down – in this way they journey to us from the stars, never from the bottom up, the way plants grow.

'Look, there is gold all around when she speaks': After reading 'The Three Little Men in the Woods', children understood that ugly words used by a child caused toads to be everywhere, but beautiful words scattered the world with gold.

'Not a single raindrop is ever lost': Where has this raindrop been? Mother Earth is very protective of her children, and raindrops are always on wonderful adventures here and there, but never lost.

Since the world of the fairy tale belongs to the child, elevating one to that reality makes a stronger connection with the world of the imagination. We as teachers are there to provide opportunities for the Kindergarten child to expand her imagination. One way was to provide a rich environment filled with beautiful, picturesque words.

What has Shaped my Life?

Beauty

My father's strong love and admiration for me opened up avenues for inner beauty that I wish for every daughter.

I am indebted to my mother for my great passion for beauty. One of my most early remembrances is when she would bundle us up in her great new Dodge and take us to fields and fields of poppies. The Los

Angeles hills were ablaze with the vivid colour of golden poppies, with lupines showing here and there. We gathered them in our arms, looked into their faces, put them in our hair, and sat surrounded with their fragrance as we breathed in their beauty. Every Spring we spent days and days in this beauty that was ours, all ours. We brought home baskets full to spread around the neighbourhood.

My mother always had plenty of help in raising her children. Besides, my grandmother, it seems, was always there when we needed her. Therefore my days were spent in play. Hour after hour I would play with the beautiful silks that belonged to my Aunt Dorothy, the dancer, who studied with Isadora Duncan. I would wrap myself and pose and dance in front of the full-length mirror that was in my bedroom. The feel and love of these beautiful materials are mine to this day. The beauty of the colours still lingers with me.

My Aunt Dorothy was an artist. She was the first one that I ever saw with brush and paint. I remember going to her apartment and watching as she created a charming picture on a card with her water colours. Her pictures and cards were beautiful. My own mother had done china painting before her marriage but I never saw her paint, but she did crochet. My grandmother was the one who sewed. I have to this day some of the beautiful dresses of velvet, silk, and chiffon that my grandmother made for me.

My grandmother, Lillian Knapp, had a beautiful garden in Berkeley, where she lived. It was pure joy for me to be there at age seven and it was there I first fell in love with the colour, fragrance, and texture of all plants. I remember catching bees in the lavender Canterbury bells. I remember taking long walks with her through the eucalyptus trees, gathering the leaves to bring them home for tea. My love and feeling of connectedness to the earth in all its awe and beauty started from these moments in Berkeley.

My mother, much too busy with her Eastern Star activities, six children, church, and nature trips, was only too willing to let me be in charge of the garden! It was a corner lot – my joy! My Aunt Marcella helped me by providing plants and suggestions.

Sometime later on, my birthday, perhaps my eighth or ninth year, I was given a gift of love and great beauty. I remember my brothers, Al and Bud, in the breakfast nook leaning over the table and saying, 'How lucky you are', but they did not give the secret away. My grandmother had set up in the den a beautiful bedroom for me with a complete bedroom set (French) with every possible accessory that one could dream of. I wish that just once in the life of every child such a gift of surprised joy could be given.

My mother was a great lover of adventure – in fact I can never remember her being home. We were always away on trips – to the beach, to the mountains, fishing, hiking in Griffith Park. I learned to love nature and its beauties from my mother and her mother. Because I know the value of feeling an adult's passion and love of the earth, I have given my life to fostering this in the children that have been placed in my care. Some years ago I wrote my Doctor of Education Practicum Report on 'Cultivating Beauty in an Integrated Aesthetic Program that Meets the Needs of the Child'. I am grateful that beauty fills my life everyday.

Literature and Literacy

My grandmother told me all the fairy tales and nursery rhymes. Lucky is the child who contains all these words of ancient wisdom. I, in turn, would become the story-teller for my brothers and sisters. I remember the day I learned to read. I, too, believe along with John Steinbeck that 'It is perhaps the greatest single effort that the human undertakes, and he must do it as a child'.

I remember the day I carried my paperback book home to read to my mother when I was in the first grade. I had learned to read. The excitement of this anticipation of being able to read to my mother is still with me. In my memory, we sat down together not far from the front door. I read the entire book to her with great delight and joy. When I was finished, she said to me, 'Now read it backwards!'. With more joy than before, I read the entire book backwards. It was at that moment that I had the feeling of coming into my own. I had become more than I had thought myself to be. Now, I would use the word 'transcended' for this occasion, for now I knew what my mother could not know. I, and I alone, knew this wonderful secret: I had learned to read. I didn't need a celebration; learning to read was celebration enough.

When my grandchild Sarah learned to read, I asked if a picture of her reading to her sister, Merina, could be placed in the children's room at our village library in celebration of her learning to read. The picture was hung celebrating one of the most important steps of life that just happens to fall in childhood.

It was the library in Los Angeles near our house that nourished my love of literature. My mother would read to me. We would read to the last minute that the book was due and then I would rush off to the library on my skates, always alone. But it was Mrs Laverne Perrin, my seventh-grade teacher at Bel Pasi School, who introduced me to the great literature of the world. We had to learn a poem each week. She would read Sir Walter Scott's work, and in a different vein, 'Uncle Tom's Cabin' was one where we hung onto every word. She read us, I am sure, all the things she loved, for I remember her great passion in the love of these books. Each story was more than its words: It was the whole realm of history, culture, nature, philosophy, religion, and psychology. Because of this heritage, I now read, and re-read from several books a day, all of which I own in my library, a tribute to these foundation years when I was loved by them and given what these darlings had been given in their youth and now were able to give to me.

Reading is one of the most important events in the life of a human being, and it happens in childhood. Have you ever thought of all the skills that must come together to be able to read? This exciting event that places the human being above all forms of life is a gift of the gods. What we do with this gift determines who we are, and as a teacher I feel privileged to help parents of the Kindergartners build the foundation for productive citizens who grow up loving to read. I hope that celebrations and ritual can be built up around the event when a child of today learns to read. It has taken us this long to realize that this is a magical moment that needs recognition.

Awe and Wonder

During the Depression, when having land seemed a burden, we moved from the city to my father's ranch. Moving to the ranch was like moving to heaven – the world opened up on every level. One such level was the night sky. We slept on hay wagons that were brought in from the fields piled high with hay. No one expected the amazing sight of such a black sky caught up in the Milky Way, and I felt myself a part of this enveloping universe that I had never experienced before. Living in the city, I had never seen a night sky. The dazzle of the millions of stars and shooting stars every night brought me into pure connection with awe and wonderment. I studied astronomy in college, and I now know that there are more than three hundred billion stars. I have experienced this great Milky Way Galaxy that surrounds our earth and carries us around the sun at the speed of 180 miles each second. Delighting in play with one's imagination, there seemed no end to the sensation of being one with the universe while floating within this Galaxy.

The awe and majesty of California's sunsets were thrilling. If no other beauty had filled my life, those sunsets would have been enough. I became one with the glorious colour and design of each sunset. Of course I now know it was because of the dust that such vibrant colour filled our lives – and isn't this the way it should be? To turn the dust of this world into beauty just as the great myth of creation when God formed man out of the dust: this same clay that formed our bodies has been here since the beginning of creation. We are older than we know, and the awe of this great gesture fills me with gratitude.

Part VII

Parents and School Proper

'Homework' for Parents

1. Every night, read to your child the stories told in our Kindergarten. I make it my job to see that you (parents) have a copy of each week's story. This comes home in your child's story book that she has dictated herself. Read or tell them as many times as it takes until your own child can tell them back to you. There is not time during our Kindergarten day for me to hear your child tell each story. I wish for the stories to live with you and your family during the year. These stories are the 'religion' of the child, and embedded in them is the wisdom that we carry to the grave! When your child is having a rough time, tell her stories from your heart that relate in story form to the situation using animals, plants, or whatever brings clarity to the moment.

2. Perhaps you could begin having your own puppet shows at home.

3. Please see that it is your Kindergarten child who inventories all household items. This should be kept as a serious document in your household files. We are now learning to use this 'language of the universe'. We want it to be used for meaningful endeavours.

4. Please send to school important numbers from your family's background on 3 x 6 inch paper. Some examples are: Grandfather lived for 98 years; there are 2,000 grapevines on our hills. We will build these numbers in class. The number should be written on one side of the paper, and the description of the number on the other side.

5. On separate pieces of paper, write each of the letters we learn. Choose the best one and send it to someone whose name starts with that letter, whose business starts with that letter, and so on.

6. Make the alphabet with weatherproof material and put it in appropriate places in the garden.
7. Make a printing press using weather stripping to form letters on tin cans. Put poster paint on these letters and print.
8. Start your own Kindergarten book and fill it with our stories, poems, and songs, as well as photographs of our activities.
9. Write stories and illustrate them.
10. Give your child time to dream.
11. Provide dress-ups and enough space to dramatize events and stories.
12. Make a song book illustrating our songs.
13. Bake with your child. One day this week I came home to find a handful of children baking in my kitchen. They were radiant with joy. Some had never kneaded dough before.
14. Play....
15. Play with a friend from Kindergarten.
16. Draw pictures with honey crayons as a family, or let the child draw by himself.
17. Visit places where people are doing 'the world's work'. Your child is in her imitative years, and she needs to settle in and choose what calls her name. She must 'try on' the culture in every form of honest work.
18. Post her jobs, which will help the family run smoothly. See that she has the proper tools to do her jobs.
19. Begin preparation of Valentine-making in the New Year. (There are no bought cards in Room 7.) He will need to make one Valentine for each child in Kindergarten with a special gift attached, such as gum, a nut, or a cookie. He should also bring in to class in the first week of February a 12-inch-wide decorated box with a large slit in the top to hold his Valentines. With this activity goes the need to be able to read all the names of the children in the class. Please put their names on cards and let him play with them this week.
20. Let him choose one of his toys to give away to someone less fortunate than he is.
21. Plan your spring garden.
22. Put puppets in a basket and take them to someone who needs to hear a child tell a story.
23. Find a Community Garden and work together as a family or twosome. This makes it possible for children who have no gardens

to see vegetables growing, and so on.

24. Make a list of home duties and read them from the list, or post the list for the week.
25. Fill the days of your life with song, poetry, dance, art, and music.
26. Take time for naps, both young and old.
27. Build a tree house.
28. Build a place for sand play.
29. Always say 'yes' before you say 'no'.
30. Take scheduled trips to the library, farm, museums, and mentors for your child.

The Kindergarten's Place within the School

What is the relationship between the Kindergarten and school proper? – for connect they surely must. What I call 'The Listening Ear' is a part of my classroom. It is the connection between our room and the school office – which some people call 'the intercom'. I want the children to know that if we are in trouble, someone is always listening. All we need do is ask for help, and they are ready to help us.

I always tell the children in advance when I need to speak to the Listening Ear. 'Children, I will talk now to the Listening Ear. Room 7, Room 7', I call, although at the office a light from our room flashes on and bells ring to tell them who is calling. I do not need to say Room 7, but I want to establish myself by identifying ourselves. I do this by saying our room number. Of course the Kindergarten room number just happens in our school to be 7 – the perfect number.

When at times it is necessary to call our secretary, the entire room goes into a ghostly quiet that seems to acknowledge the awe of the magnificence of the moment we all take for granted, the mystery of one room talking to another. At this age, they are just feeling the magic of talking to each other; and now here we all are, involved in linking ourselves with the office, asking for vital information. I say, 'Michelle is not here in school. Is she going to be late?'

Whenever we have important news in the Kindergarten, it is spread throughout the school – something we do in several different ways. As the year goes by, the signs carrying our news get larger and larger; by spring, our signs about the eggs that are about to hatch reach poster size. Each child takes her poster to a place in the school that she feels would be the very best place for it to be displayed. It is the public display that demands her best: everyone is aware of her important task, and the quality of work transcends even what she thought was her very best.

Every celebration we have in the Kindergarten finds us dressed in costumes that help celebrate the day. We parade through the rooms in the school carrying our banners, flags, and so on, singing as we go, with our violinist normally leading the way. At Christmas we all ring bells as we go from class to class. We announce Spring each year throughout the school: we dress in our Spring costumes, singing, 'Spring is here! Spring is here!' Of course, I do make arrangements with the teachers, but as we go along we find other doors flung open to welcome us.

We call the new principal 'the Princess'. When the class first gathers, we plan our trip to her castle and take her a golden crown. Of course, she is delighted with this admiration, and the children continue to call her the Princess throughout the year. She keeps her crown on her shelf for all to see, and she wears it when she comes to visit us.

I do not, under any circumstances, allow the Kindergarten children to be in the evening programmes that the school puts on. In the life of each child there must be signposts that state his progress in growing up. The Kindergarten child can look forward to these school programmes as a member of another class when he leaves Kindergarten. We have many programmes where the child's skills can be developed. Our Kindergarten programmes are always held during our school days, 8:30 to 2:10; we have our own timing.

At the close of the year, we use our printing press to make the numbers of each room in the school. We deliver these to the room and put them in an envelope I have attached to each door. If the class has 22 children, then we know we must make 22 signs using their room number. These numbers are gifts to the children in the other grades, to remember their room numbers.

I feel it is important to enter into the life of the school in small steps. The Kindergarten children have their own play garden. They come directly through our garden gate each morning into the classroom. We do not see the other part of the school during the school day.

The secretary is always a special friend of the Kindergarten child.

Claudia, our secretary, is honoured by us on her birthday, and the celebration is held in our Kindergarten room. On special occasions we decorate her desk and room. School secretaries are saints, and should be treated so.

I feel it is the job of the Kindergarten teacher to train the principal and the superintendent in the Kindergarten lore. They need to see through the eyes of the Kindergarten teacher how she prepares to meet the needs of the children. This, I feel, is a duty that is part of the job; it cannot be left undone. They must know why there should be only 20 children in the Kindergarten and no more. They must realize that the quality of material is altogether as important as the quantity – the best of material should be found in the Kindergarten.

They must know that the Kindergarten teacher does not take on extra duties, such as yard duty to watch children other than her own, for she is *always* on duty with her own children and their parents. They must know that the janitorial duties are more extensive in the Kindergarten; and the janitor hired must be one who feels his self-worth, a saint who is an example of a warm human being whom we can honour. They must know the value of a garden outside the Kindergarten door. The administration must know that all of life's lessons are learned in the garden. They must be prepared to help in any way needed. They must see that money for the Kindergarten is available, for we do not use textbooks, etc. The money that is given to other grades must equal the money given to the Kindergarten. Our needs must be met; and it is the Kindergarten teacher who makes this clear.

I feel a teacher must train the administration, just as she does her school parents. They must know that a Kindergarten teacher is her own programme and doesn't need outside programmes bought by the school. She is her own music programme; she is her science programme, and so on. We all want to do our best, whether we are superintendents or teachers. And it is up to the Kindergarten teacher to see that the superintendent, the principal, and the board of trustees are given the training so that they will feel comfortable with the world of the five-year-old. Actually, I feel that the administration and teachers should all be on the same salary scale; I see no difference in our responsibilities.

The role of the Kindergarten teacher means that she must be aware of all research that affects the life of the child. This means she knows what nourishes the brain at this stage of development; she knows that the child requires human models, touching, and eye contact that machines such as computers do not and never can provide. Because play is so vital to childhood, there must be room and equipment both inside and outside to enrich this activity.

The teacher must constantly seek out mentors who are knowledgeable about the lawful development of the child. She must be aware of the literature that would serve to train the parents and the administrators so they can understand the richness of the Kindergarten programme.

General Issues

Multiple modalities are being encouraged in the curriculum. Parents are invited to participate in the education of their children in the classroom by volunteering during the day and by attending parent evenings dealing with various Kindergarten topics. The diverse cultural and religious backgrounds of the children play an important role in determining the flavour of the curriculum and festivals.

♦   There is room for spontaneity.
♦   Children's ideas are used.
♦   Transitions flow in artistic ways.
♦   Conflicts are respected and resolved as a learning process.
♦   Manners are taught and practised.
♦   The Kindergarten revolves around the philosophy that all things are all things.
♦   Chaos is understood.

Part VIII

Endings and Loss

Death in the Kindergarten

We live in the balance of death and life. We come from the land of life, the womb, into the land of death, so it must seem when we leave that place near the mother's heart where music, food, warmth, and our little 'hot tub' were pure bliss; to be thrown out of this paradise into a shocking death, which seems, perhaps, worse than death, which has miraculously become LIFE.

We learn as we grow older that death, having been cheated of its victim, has ways of claiming us. One of the ways is negativity; others are fear, lack of concern, and so on. If, however, we can learn to live passionate lives of meaning and wholeness, our fear of death vanishes. But the question remains: How do we handle the subject of death as parents and teachers of small children?

When my children were small, we lived next door to my husband's three aunts. Willys' parents also lived around the corner from us. My parents lived on a ranch nearby in the San Joaquin Valley, and visited us often. They were all in their 70s. At the time 70 seemed quite old. Of course, now it doesn't seem at all old. However, I felt that any day we could lose them and I thought of ways of preparing my children for their deaths. I explained that when one died, it meant that a person now could go anywhere they liked. Of course, loving adventure and travel, they thought this was wonderful. One day I heard Bill say to Ann as they were playing up in Ann's room, 'Let's die and go to the ranch'. On another day when we were visiting an elderly widow, Bill looked around her room at the old Saratoga Inn and said, 'Where is your daddy?' 'Oh, he died', she said. Then Bill said, 'Where did he go?', a question she had hardly ever asked herself, I'm sure. When the daughter of our children's doctor died, I made great preparation to tell them that she had died while planting seeds in the garden. I wanted them to experience the great lesson of the garden, that is, 'Life into death and death into life'.

I wish to share my experience of handling death in the years I taught in Kindergarten. During my 45 years as a Kindergarten teacher, I, like every teacher, found ways of giving comfort to those in need. During my beginning years of teaching, I myself had not yet come to terms with death, when the first child in my Kindergarten died after an accident at home. He ran into the garage door on his bicycle. The best way of dealing with it that I knew at that time was to give a book with the child's name to the library and send a handwritten note to the family saying how sorry I was.

By the time the second child met with an accident on a snow trip, I was able to be of more help to the family. Dale's father had taken the family to the snow so that the mother could have some time to get well from the 'flu'. It was the day before we were to celebrate Saint Valentine's day. On that Monday morning, school was told of the tragedy. I felt it important for me to visit with Dale's parents before I told the Kindergarten children.

When it was time for the party to begin, we sat around in a circle and passed out the remaining Valentines. Most of them had already been placed in our Saint Valentine boxes. Every child received one from Dale. At the end of the day I collected all of Dale's Valentines from his empty place in the circle and rushed out of the door along with the children. I took them to his home where the family had gathered. We read and cried together as we looked at them all. I told his family all about his days in Kindergarten. I told them I wanted to plant a flowering tulip tree outside the Kindergarten door. I said that when I had found the right one I would call them and we would all plant it together. It had to be just his height. Dale was the shortest one in the Kindergarten, but he always walked as though he was ten feet tall.

And so the tree has grown that tall and blooms every year around Saint Valentine's day. I now go each autumn and collect pods from this tree to use for the lesson on the umbilical cord. Someone at the school long after I moved to another school planted more of these trees, making a long row between the buildings. But Dale's tree is the first. It is the first tree you see as you open the Kindergarten door where he had his few short days as a Kindergarten child.

Sometime later his mother brought me a lovely oil painting that she and Dale had painted together. He sat by her side as she painted this picture of the first Saratoga school. It is a picture of the first school house built in our town with all the children out in front with the teacher. It hung in my schoolroom as long as I taught Kindergarten. It now hangs in my kitchen and we will celebrate 150 years of our school in 2004/2005. I feel all the layers of love and tragedy that are woven together in that picture when I look at it.

Through the years I learned to honour death in more meaningful ways when it became a part of my life. It was I who was growing into the wholeness of life in all its mysterious ways so that I became more of a help to the parents and the children. Also I was able to feel the healing process in a more profound way myself.

The healing that needs to take place when a child dies must come to us all. It is sometimes the first experience parents have had with death, let alone the first time for the children in the Kindergarten class to be confronted with the death of a classmate. I learned to share with these parents of young children the deaths in my family. I began to help celebrate the lives and deaths of grandparents with the children and all those they felt dear. We talked about death often in the Kindergarten; the garden gave us this opportunity. In the garden it is always 'death into life and life into death'. We always found that death made way for life and life for death. They could grasp this in the planting of the seed. A seed contains the mysteries of birth, and yet it must also reckon with death by being buried in the ground. We honoured the 'Return to the Earth Bucket' by putting all the leftover crumbs in it. It was the mother of Andreas who brought our first earth bucket to our room. We collected crumbs along with all the leaves for our compost pile. We used the new soil from the compost in spring for our garden. We knew how fragile the plants in our garden were and what happened to them when we were careless. These were small steps in the cycle of life, but steps we were actively involved with every day in the garden.

I used the animals that we found that had died. We were always finding dead birds in the garden, which offered an opportunity for sadness, appreciation, awe, rejoicing in the gift of birds, and in the life of this particular bird. We would make up stories about what that bird had seen and done during its lifetime. We would have a procession with signs and songs carrying the bird to its special place in our garden. This grave had been dug with great care, and then the ceremony would begin. In this way I felt perhaps we were paving the way for later times when death would be part of our lives on another level.

But all the songs, poems, stories, and processions that we would use for these occasions did not prepare us or make Devon's death easier. Never had a child been this sick in my Kindergarten and never had we heard of this new disease called Reyes Syndrome. As soon as the office told me she was in the hospital, I wrote to the Kindergarten parents.

What does a teacher do who hears that one of the children in the Kindergarten is in Intensive Care? As soon as I heard Devon was in the hospital, Jason Taylor and I rushed to the Community Garden and picked flowers – fragile beauty that seems only for the moment – reflecting our own lifetime we take so for granted, and yet made from the same substances, knowing our same nights and days. They are very, very like us and yet very different. Flowers – gifts of the universe – seem so like the gift of a child that it always seems right that they be brought together. We left them at the family's door, for no one was home. The next day I stopped by the house and left a note.

Tonight Devon Deming's grandmother called me to say that the flu had turned into a very rare disease, Reyes Syndrome, that affects both the brain and liver. Devon has been in a coma since Friday and is now, among many other serious steps, on a breathing machine. I wrote the following note to the parents of the Kindergarten children:

Dear Devon,

I took you so for granted when you came through that door every morning with your hugs and kisses and gifts that you had made for all of us, and with your bubbly self loving us all. You were the very first to draw so many pictures that started the week's new sound. With each new sound your smile took on a glow that soon filled us all. It was as though doors were opening up on every level of relatedness; there was no limit. The world was yours, and because you were able to do it, our little group had caught the whole spirit of this adventure of putting life's pieces together into what we call reading.

You and I have sat beside each other in the Golden Ring since school began, and tomorrow I shall miss your singing of 'Good Morning, Mrs Betty Peck'. When I greet everyone tomorrow, I shall be a different person because of you. I shall see these fragile gifts of the moment with an alive joyfulness and gratitude deep within that I was privileged to know you – the true light of childhood, age five – who had been kissed by the gods.

The devastating days ahead for this little family will need all of us listening to our own hearts to learn how to help with the healing of this tragedy that has come to us all.

Hugs,

bp

Each day we sent a large mural for her hospital room. The bed was always drawn first. Then surrounding the bed were flowers everywhere with Devon's face peeking through. The next day, it was the hospital bed with angels dancing everywhere on the bed, the walls, the ceiling with Devon peeking through. Each child made their own flowers, cut them out, and pasted them on the mural, which was sent to the hospital each day.

Several days later, after the children had gone home, I was called down to the office to hear what we had all feared. When I went back to the room some parents were still there and I asked if they wanted me to tell the children that Devon had died. They all agreed it would be best if they all knew it at once and could come home and tell their parents. So after school the next day I wrote another letter to the Kindergarten parents:

Dears:

I am writing this at the close of the day, February 26, 1980. Yesterday when all the children had gone, Bunny called and told me that she had spoken to Devon's mother. I looked around the room and knew what had to be done. All our songs, poetry, stories, and singing games from the beginning of school would be needed to help us through the day. The letter of the week was 'U'. I had told the story of the letter 'U' with pictures of raindrops coming down to earth, staying awhile, and then being called back up by the sun. At first I had painted a picture of the rain clouds letting all the raindrops out to play. Then the sun was seen gathering all the raindrops back, riding on the golden path you sometimes see. We stood on the ledge of our shelf under our beautiful windows that framed the leafless catalpa tree and acted out the story of the raindrops.

On this day I knew that the raindrops must turn into angels. I took out the paints and painted a picture of angels descending to the earth, trailing across the earth and then up into the sky again. 'All that comes down must go up' had become required learning. I filled the room with flowers and saw that the angel costumes were in order.

We talked about the picture of 'U', and we reminded ourselves how all the letters are gifts of the stars. They follow the path down to the earth, like the letter U, down across the earth line, and up. We looked at the rainbows we had painted on Monday. Finding that one rainbow didn't go all the way across the sky, but had stopped in a cloud so the fairies could get off, Scott said, 'Oh, is that how people get to heaven?'.

'Yes', I said, we could change the raindrops to angels. And so we did; and now instead of being raindrops we were ready to get into our costumes and have the play about this letter in a new way. Everyone wore bits of white netting and lace curtains, and climbed up to our golden curtain on the window ledge. We prepared the rainbow bridge (our classroom boat turned over to make steps). This was covered with scarves of every rainbow hue placed in rainbow order.

Then all was ready for the announcer to strike the bell. When the last circle of sound had spread out over the world, the play was announced. The play's new name was 'Angels Coming Down to Earth'. It was only yesterday that we were 'Raindrops Coming Down to Earth'.

Then we all came down, descending over the rainbow bridge. We all played on the earth for a while, then Rosemary, my aide, who was the angel who stayed 'on high' to call out our names, called out our names one by one when it was time to go back over the rainbow bridge to the sky. When everyone was back home safe, the bell sounded and the play was over.

'Again!', they all called. Then still again.... Just one more time. Never had the children wanted to repeat a play so many times. Then we all took sky-blue paper and drew ourselves coming and going over the rainbow bridge. 'U' had become part of us in many ways.

It was 'teacher time' next, and we gathered in small groups to make our Magic Doors, which was followed by butterfly-making. We make Magic Doors every week, for each letter. The doors open up to show all things that surround the letter of the week. The letter of the week is written on two paper doors with stars above, showing where all the letters come from. On Monday we had heard the story of the caterpillar, and now we folded paper and centred the body of the butterfly along the fold. Then we put drops of paint on one side. We closed the paper and pressed it so that the magic of the wings could be seen when we opened it. I helped my group cut paper-doll angels, holding hands, from white paper. Then it was playtime in the garden. The room was dark when they were called in to build their nests. We sang our quiet songs as we rested.

At this time, I fixed a circle of ribbon and netting with a wreath of smilax that held a lighted candle. The girls were called first, and then the boys. Here we were all gathered together in the Golden Ring, ready to listen to the fairy tale. The story was about an angel who came to earth on her own five-pointed star, gathering rainbow colours as she came. Down she came into the arms of the most beautiful mother and the strongest and dearest father in the world whom she had chosen for her very own. As she grew older on the earth, she could feel the place where her wings had been. Each day she gave angel hugs and smiles and songs to everyone she knew. Then came the day she heard the wind fairies calling her name. First it was just a faint call, and then it seemed that all the fairies and angels were calling: 'Come home... come home....' She picked herself up without even saying goodbye and was off over the rainbow bridge.

After the story, we went for a walk, and as we passed the great oak tree,

Beth discovered that the flag was half-way down on the pole. 'Oh, when the flag is half-way down, it tells us that someone has died', I said. 'It must be Devon', the children answered. 'Yes, the flag tells us that Devon has died', I said, 'and tomorrow when we see the flag it shall again touch the golden ball at the top'.

We would be using the great 'U' symbol over and over again, but never would it touch our lives as it did this day.

We hurried back through the garden gate, filled with questions that have no answers. The afternoon children went off to have their lunch, and the morning children picked forget-me-nots to take home. Around the flowers were the paper angels holding hands carrying the message of the day: 'Devon, five years old for ever.' I imagined Devon free to express for ever the spirit of her five-year-old spontaneous, joyous Spirit of discovery.

Jenni came to have lunch with the afternoon children. As I came through the garden gate, she said, 'We found a note from Devon'. All the children came running up, telling us that Jonathan had found a message from Devon in the garden. We all gathered around as I held the pink paper kissed by the rain and the sun. Yes, it was Devon's. There was her name with her 'N' marching along in the other direction. We could see all her favourite words: 'To Mom, To Dad, Love, Devon'. This little pink paper had waited until this day to be found. And John said, 'She must have dropped it on her way'.

When the afternoon children left for home, they picked their blue forget-me-not bouquets and put their paper angels holding hands dancing around the flowers, and on each was written the message of the day: 'Devon, five years old for ever.'

Hugs,

bp

On the following day, I again wrote a note to the parents:

Dears,

We picked all the flowers in our garden on Wednesday, and we have them ready to take to Devon's family this morning, along with all her Kindergarten treasures. After we had had our angel parade singing, 'All Night, All Day' with the angels we had made, we let them fly from the balcony.

As soon as we were back inside, Sarti's mother came in with cupcakes, saying she couldn't think of a better place to celebrate her thirtieth birthday than with us in the Kindergarten. So she sat down amongst all the flowers we had picked, and we sang 'Happy Birthday' and made her surprise pictures for her birthday book. We pulled the curtains, closing out the sun, and sat in candlelight celebrating life in the midst of death.

Hugs,

bp

The next day, I told the children that Devon's family had all gathered together to celebrate her life and that our garden flowers were part of that celebration. And now it was our turn. How shall we celebrate her life? Without any hesitation, they knew exactly what had to be done. 'We shall have a party', someone said. I said that I would bring an angel food cake. 'We shall all wear costumes', said another. 'We shall have The Coming Down to Earth Angel Play', another one said. So we spent the day planning and making all that we would need for our celebration.

I realized after arriving home that there was no time for me to make an angel food cake. So I called up Bob the Baker and asked if he could not only make an angel food cake, but also whether the Kindergarten could come down and help him ice it. This cake had to be meaningful in every way and decorated in the proper and most beautiful way. 'Yes', he said, he would be glad to do it.

So all the angels in their white flowing curtains, veils, gossamer gowns, silks, and sheets went out of the garden gate. We passed between the golden safety cross, walk lines, and down the hill. Of course it was like the 'U' we had been identifying with all week. As we walked, or rather flew, upon the earth past the stores, we were stopped by the display in the jewellery store window. Here was a painted rainbow going up into the clouds. As we were admiring this amazing coincidence of finding our very own painting lesson in a new cut-out version in the window, our friend Jenni came along and asked where we were going. When she heard we were going to the bakery, she wanted to go along with us. As we were gathered around her, a huge truck came out of the alley that is next to the jewellery store. The driver would have had no idea that angels would be flying low. Nor would I suspect such a huge truck to be able to fit in the alley way.

Bob the Baker was waiting for us and ushered the angels into his 'holy of holies'. We stood around his large working table near his great ovens and admired the large un-iced angel food cake. 'Well', he said, 'how shall we decorate this cake?' 'With angels, flowers, hearts, stars, rainbows, and D's!', they shouted. And sure enough, they all began to appear on the cake. It was more than beautiful!

The moment the cake was placed in our hands, our posture changed. We walked with great dignity past the jewellery shop, up the hill, over the golden cross walk, and there, standing by the our garden gate, was a large white rabbit. It was Jonathan's mother, dressed in a white rabbit's suit. Being an artist, she felt that the 'U' had to be painted in a special way on our hands this week. She had brought her paints and dressed up in a bunny suit to surprise us. We were delighted! Now we would not only have a lovely painting on our hands with her special paints, but we would have an audience as well for our play. We moved the celebration of Devon's life outdoors. The structure became the heavens. The play began with rain coming down to the earth and being called back by the sun, then butterflies, then angels. Jonathan's mother and I cried through it all. We sang our songs and told our stories and ate our cake iced with hearts, angels, flowers, and Ds. The week came to a close, but of course it was just the beginning of a lifelong encounter with this cycle of life we call death.

We did not ever let an opportunity go by to be part of the celebration of the life of a family member who died. Even if the grandfather lived in Taiwan, this was a wonderful opportunity for us all to experience the beauty of their celebration of life when Eileen's grandfather died.

Dear Parents All:

Yes, we are having our tribute to you tomorrow, Friday, May 8th, at 11.00 a.m. You, moms, will be the queens. Our letter this week is 'M'. With our shoulders we say, mighty, magic, moving mountains… and when we say it with our lips closed, it is the letter that begins your name, mom, and it is painted on our mouths, of course.

We are giving you our gifts that we have made with our love and sewing and our garden flowers. All the mothers who have helped with our programme this year, teachers, drivers, gift senders, and dough makers, will receive gifts on that day from our special efforts through the year.

Today Eileen Tsi left with her family for Taiwan. Her 78-year-old grandfather died. We saw pictures of him dressed in his five sets of clothes: one for Spring, one for Summer, one for Winter; then over this were put his formal business clothes, dark blue and black. He will be ready now for any season to come. The final covering is a red brocade sack. This will keep his bones together so he won't have to go looking around for them (when the trumpet blows).

The class made a poster showing the four seasons as we know them here. Then we put the number of each year that he was on earth as a border around the 4 by 14 foot poster, with a flower in between the numbers. It looked beautiful.... They took it with them on the aeroplane to Taiwan.

Our red and purple Oriental poppy bloomed just in time to pick it for the special trip to celebrate the grandfather's life. We send our blessings!

Please come through our garden gate and sit in your chairs in the garden. Your child will come and sit with you after or during the programme. Then we will sing 'Come Follow Me' as we parade to the greenwood tree, carrying our gift from the earth for all to eat.

The room mothers have been so kind to plan a meeting next Tuesday night for us all to meet at the school at 7:30. I do hope you all can come. We will be talking about the meaningfulness of the Kindergarten programme and how it can enrich the lives of our families and the child's adult life to come.

Hugs,

bp

Brian's Dad

Since I now see in every death an opportunity to celebrate both life and death, as soon as I heard my Kindergarten child Brian's dad, Mike, had cancer of the pancreas, I knew there had to be immediate action in the Kindergarten. The doctor said 'two months to two years'. Lee, who is a lifelong friend of Brian's family, came to tell me, and in so doing she also brought the news that Mike's birthday was the following day, Friday. I thought it important that the Kindergarten help celebrate his birthday. Changes had to be made, since I was planning to celebrate a Kindergarten child's birthday on that day in our Kindergarten. Billy, the birthday child, was planning an after-school party for all the children that day.

Knowing that Billy's real birthday was Saturday, I decided to change that celebration we were having for him to the following week, after I talked it over with Billy and his mom. Yes, it would be all right with her and she knew it would be all right with Billy, since all he could think of was his after-school party.

A birthday has its one special day, but celebrating it may be any day before or any day afterwards. This I have said over and over again in the Kindergarten, so the children were accustomed to this practice.

Our letter of the week was 'M' – a holdover from our Mother's Day Week. Each Friday we celebrate the sound of the week. And what better way than to celebrate Mike's birthday. Never before had we had a birthday party for an adult whose name started with the sound of the week.

On Friday, our Sound Party Day, I called up Mike. What does one say to the father whose wife died of cancer the previous year and who now finds himself with cancer and the doctors having given him a limited time? When his wife died he decided to stay home with his two boys for at least a year. We have seen a good deal of Mike at school. All the children know him. He has taken on the job of fixing our broken toys.

As you know, it was because of Brian that I told the story of Cinderella – the French Perrault version of the story of the girl whose mother had died. Instead of a mother, she had a Fairy Godmother who was there when she needed her. On Mother's Day, Brian's Fairy Godmother had to be there. Their beautiful neighbour, Lee, was the one who came dressed as Brian's Fairy Godmother, bringing her wand. It was Mike who had made the lovely star wand for her out of wood. Perhaps she will think of giving it to Brian with a note that she will come and brighten it each year at this time. Or better still, to have him come over to her house for a special ceremony of renewing the star shine each year. Lucky is the child who can carry traditions of his childhood on into his later years. And how lucky it is to know someone who knew you as a child.

When Mike came to the phone, I told him that Lee had come to tell me of the cancer and how sorry I was to hear this. He said the only answer one can give: 'Well, thank you.' 'Lee also told me it was your birthday, and I am asking if the Kindergarten could help celebrate your birthday here in our classroom.' 'Yes', he said. I also said that after the party I would like to have a heart-to-heart talk with him.

So we set the time at 11 o'clock. Then the next step was to talk to his son, Brian. He must be the one to present the real invitation to his father. Would he please ask him to come at 11.00, or better, could he write the number down so that his dad would not forget?

Billy's mother said she would send the birthday cupcakes, as she was planning to make them for Billy anyway. In all the busy preparation for Billy's after-school party, Billy's dad arrived with the cupcakes for Mike.

At our parties there is an exchange of gifts. What would be the best gift we could make for Brian's dad, Mike? Of course, it would be to write down all his years. So on gold paper we all wrote from 1 to 46. The number '46' was made special in some way by each child. Some chose to make rainbows around it; some drew sparkling rays shining forth from the number; some made a border all around it, as though it were housed in its own special destiny.

Of course, into each drawing I read the secret meaning it had for me. The rainbows were saying, 'Mike, your days have been filled with all the colours that we call wholeness. Now take the gold and run with it.' Into the sparkles of the sun I read, 'There is no better ending to this life than to be caught up in the brightness of the purifying sun that is eternal life itself'. For by now I had heard that the doctors were saying it would only be two months. Two months is such a short time, but we wanted to give Brian rich memories to remember.

Lee Anne came with her violin to lead the birthday procession from the garden into the room. She has come to the Kindergarten with her wonderful music every Friday. No birthday celebration is complete without music. As we came into the room singing 'Happy Birthday', we found Brian's dad sitting on the heavy redwood logs that we had put together for a throne. On either side was a place for Brian and for Billy, the Birthday Boy. Then the children gave Mike a golden crown with 'M's' dancing around the top.

Both Brian and Billy received a crown. As we all gathered in the Golden Ring, I noticed that since last Friday, when I had last seen Mike, his weight loss was the only noticeable sign of the days ahead. His spirit was more than triumphant. He received each gift as though it were a gift that money could not buy.

All his years were collected on one side of the paper. The other side of the paper was filled with colourful decorations of flowers, rainbows, 'I love yous', and 'Happy Birthdays'. As I have emphasized elsewhere, it is so important to have real work in the Kindergarten. Numbers are the language of the universe. They are holy and are used only when real needs arise. It is the teacher's job to seize every opportunity to record this language we call Arithmetic in the Kindergarten in meaningful and beautiful ways.

But what is so wonderful about our gifts to adults and newborn babies are the wishes that accompany them. In Kindergarten we give our best wishes, as the Wise Woman (the Fairy Godmother) did for Briar Rose in the story of the Sleeping Beauty from the Brothers Grimm.

The children came to Mike one at a time and presented what they had made. Then they each gave their wish. These were written down by Heather's mother in a beautifully decorated book:

'I wish you will have a golden boat.'
'I wish you will live for ever.'
'I wish you will marry a princess.'
'I wish you will have lots of money.'
'I wish you will live in a castle.'

On and on they came, until the nineteen had had their turn pouring out their best wishes.

Mike gave each of them a cupcake in exchange. And when he did, 'thank yous' filled the air and the chimes rang out. As you know, in the Kindergarten we ring small chimes when we hear thank-yous filling the air. At the close of the gift-giving, we did some of our singing games for him. The last singing game, 'Kling Klang Gloria', took us dancing out of the room, into the garden, and off to lunch.

Birds Fly – The Last Day in Kindergarten

How does one prepare for the last day of Kindergarten? The foundations of life have been laid on every level. The growing years ahead for the Kindergarten child have been rooted in the soil of beauty, imagination, and artistic expression that will give expansion to all of literacy and numeracy.

The love of the earth has been established. The awe and wonderment of our relationship to the cosmos has filled our days. Our respect for each other's heritage and love for one another has been the essence of our Kindergarten year. Good health of our growing bodies has been introduced through cooking projects and physical exercise.

How can I say this is the last day? How can I say this is the end of school? It is only the beginning of their study of life that will lead them to becoming contributing adults in their community and thus to the world. And so I choose to say, 'This is the day the birds will fly'.

We prepare for this special day in many ways. Invitations will be sent to the parents and all those who have helped us this year. We decide to all wear blue. The blue of the sky, the blue of the birthday board for the month of June, and the blue of the forget-me-not flower that grows in our garden.

The homing pigeons arrive to live in our Kindergarten while we prepare for this day. The benches and chairs where the children will sit with their parents are placed in order. The homing pigeons are brought out. I will lead the grand singing procession through the lower door out under the catalpa tree.

After we sing our songs and do our singing games about birds that we have learned for the occasion, the children go to sit with their parents. After I have reviewed the year, I reach into my white basket that I have used all my teaching years. In this basket are all the loaves of bread that we have made and have been saving in our freezer – loaves which have been wrapped beautifully by the children.

I call each parent and helper up and thank them for all their help during our Kindergarten year and present them with a loaf of bread. Even the parents who have not helped get a loaf of bread. I say, 'The sun shines on the just and the unjust, and I know that if they had had time they would have helped in our class'.

Then I sit in my 'Goodbye Chair' that I have used all year when I give them a hug 'goodbye' each day. As I sing their name, I reach into baskets filled with gifts for them. One is a heart of gold. 'Never forget your heart of gold', I say as we give each other an arms-around-the-neck hug.

My aide and I go over to the pigeon cage where two pigeons are taken out. We each hold one. Then I speak to the pigeons as though I were speaking to a Kindergarten child: 'You have been well taken care of. You have been well fed. You have been loved. You have been given the best of everything we have. And now it is your turn to try your wings and fly.' As the birds are released, I sing 'Fly away my birds, fly away, oh fly away, oh fly away', until the last child and his parents have gone through the Garden Gate and left by foot, bicycle, or car.

FLY AWAY MY BIRDS

Betty Peck

Fly a- way my birds. Fly a- way.   Oh, fly a- way. Oh, fly a- way.

The Teacher Retires:
The Alpha and Omega Party

Just how does one announce one's retirement? Certainly not by signing a piece of paper sent out by the district office that says,

> *Pick one of the following:*
> ☐ I plan to return.
> ☐ I wish to talk it over.
> ☐ I plan to retire.

Never! This is a moment of great celebration, and I intended to make mine the most beautiful and spectacular of all retirement announcements.

First there were the invitations, which would, of course, be hand-printed. My husband has a printing press, and it is here that he hand-sets the type. It has taken us days to decide how we want the words arranged: I had wanted the word 'announcement' to appear somewhere on the invitation, but he only had a decorated M, B, or C; so I decided to use the 'C'. The word 'announcement' was cast aside for 'celebration'. Celebration seemed the perfect word to use with the letter 'C', but how was one to state that this was the beginning of the end? I decided that calling it my 'Alpha and Omega party' would bluntly state my retirement. Of course, I would hold it in my beautiful garden outside my Kindergarten door – this gave me a chance to call it a garden party.

The decision of where to hold the party was not hard to make, since the Kindergarten garden itself was ablaze with bloom. The purple wisteria would be at its best, covering the corners of the garden house and climbing the sycamores. The old roses and jasmine would be adventuring out.

And now the decision of the colour for the invitations had to be made: Should it match my dress?; should it be the colour the most nourishing to the young child, light peach? It was not until I found myself in the store confronted by all the colours that I knew immediately that it had to be lavender. Purple has always been the underlying colour of the Easter season. Purple candles are now a part of setting the mood of the season at our house, changing to white on Easter day. The purple wisteria floods the garden. Today we associate this colour with royalty, with power, and with having reached the height of all. It is also the last and final colour in the rainbow. I am often amazed at the rightness of colour that in itself sets the mood for celebration.

And now that the colour of the paper and the composition had been decided upon, the style of the type had to be chosen. Willys chose the same type he had used for our daughter's wedding invitation. It takes a true lover of hand-set type who put his heart and soul into the forming of the printed word. It is always a thrill to hear the song of this press and see the magic of the printing press take form before your eyes. There it was, the reality of the dream. As I looked at the wet ink, I realized that the next step had arrived.

The choosing of names that were to be written on the envelope would not be easy – whom to invite? A few moments were given over to thoughts of protocol, but not for long. I knew exactly whom I wanted to be there: I wanted the parents of the children with whom, over the years, for some reason or another, I have maintained a meaningful relationship. I wanted this to be an opportunity to say 'thank you' for letting me be a part of their lives. I especially wanted to thank those who had helped to create the Kindergarten garden and those whose talents had been given to make the Kindergarten room itself a sanctuary for the preservation of childhood.

I wanted to invite the parents of this class that I now have, which will be my last class – 19 wonderful families. Would there be room for the faculty of our school and the Kindergarten teachers of the district? No matter what, they too had to be invited.

The invitations, printed, addressed, and mailed the same day, which were months overdue, were mailed at the stroke of midnight. I was planning an announcement party in late autumn, but my sister Jan's cancer returned and my time was spent with her when I wasn't deep into my book. It was this autumn that, for the first time, I hired a secretary to work with me on the first draft of the book which you are now reading, titled, *Kindergarten Education: Freeing children's creative potential*. As you have seen, it tells of the programme that has evolved over the years to nourish the parent and child on every level.

But now the moment of this day had arrived. Eric's family came and filled the garden with yellow pansies and golden jasmine. During the morning my aide, Doris Dooley, had helped the leprechauns hide the piles of gold for the children in the yellow pansies.

The architect must be first on the invited list – he will be the first to be honoured. The dear maintenance manager, Henry Clarke, had to have a special invitation, for he was the one whom I called whenever the overpowering needs were not met by anyone else. Willys, of course, who has left his genius on every piece of equipment in the room, seen and unseen, must be there. The *San Jose Mercury News* would have to wait for his arrival. My daughter, who has been my inspiration since we both started Kindergarten in the Saratoga district together, I as a teacher, she as a student, must also have a special invitation. My son, Bill, would have a special invitation.

I would ask the Piper of Spring to come and greet everyone in the garden house with music as they entered. He has been the Piper of Spring each year in our garden. All of the people who had helped me with the garden itself would be invited. However, I planned to honour those who helped me by having some brass plaques made, one for each door.

On Saturday I went through the phone book and called engravers. I found an engraver who would make a brass plaque while I waited. I rushed to his crowded, cluttered shop with cats eating out of dishes on the counter. Everything had to be right, right down to what I was to wear. The fashion of the moment has always been important to me, but more so the colour, texture, and sense of history that one brings to the day. Roses have taken over the season this spring, and so my dress had to be filled with roses – I chose to use the roses my sister Jan had made. In Kindergarten one always refers to 'Spring Green' at this moment of the year when new life appears; and since I am taking steps in the direction of a 'new life', the dress had to be 'Spring Green'. Every

Kindergarten teacher knows the magic that can appear if there are pockets, and so all my dresses, including this one, are made with pockets.

What food would be the best of all to serve? At all our Kindergarten parties we serve the food that starts with the sound of the week. So now the garden party was no different. For Alpha we would have apples, the first mythical fruit, and oatmeal cookies for Omega. I ordered Spring Green apples.

After the children left at 2:20, the room had to be rearranged. I asked some of the sixth-grade boys to help me arrange the furniture in the room to give the right mood. Mrs Dooley hung streamers in the garden. The children had done their spring cleaning that day – each child was responsible for shining a small area. While cleaning, some of the children had found a note from Lady Spring, saying that she was coming after the spring cleaning. She had left the violet water to help us with our work.

When all had gathered, I rang the bells and sang 'Gather Together', as I have done to call the children in all these years, to welcome the guests inside. As I looked into the faces of families and friends, I began by saying:

'I want you to know that in this Kindergarten, an artist's work is never done, but we must find a "stopping place", a stopping place to give us space in the rhythm of life to gather our forces together for a new beginning. I want to tell you that I have found my stopping place amongst all the work that is yet to be done. And so I have called this, the celebration of the Alpha and the Omega, the Beginning and the End.'

I told the whole story of how Marv Steinberg, then the principal of this school, asked me to come over and start a Kindergarten programme at this school. 'No', I said, 'not unless I can have a garden and an oven'. 'Yes, of course', he said. 'I want it to be the best. Everything you would like. You will design the room.'

Warren Heid and I worked out ways to use the space for all that would be needed to provide the environment for a rich experience for the Kindergarten child. Everything, that is, except the floor. Today I want all those who have helped me with the room itself to have a gift that is part of this room. Behind the door to the magic cupboard is a mirror. Around this mirror, which is hand-painted with wild grasses, flowers, quail, and rabbits by Craig's mother, is written my philosophy of life: 'Thank you for every magic moment that makes it possible for me to stand here and feel how wonderful I am.' I have stood many a child here and looked into this mirror. And the adults who have stood here with me have, I think, felt the magic of this moment.

I had ten little replica mirrors made as gifts: I presented one first to Warren Heid: 'The floor is always redeemed when the catalpa tree turns its leaves this very colour'. The one to Henry Clarke, who had at one time or another fixed everything in the room, I presented saying, 'Henry, if ever you should forget how wonderful you are, this mirror will remind you'. And then one to dear Theresa Robinson, who made the Birthday Banner and also created the Mother's Lap (see pp. 14-15); a gift of the small door of the magic cupboard to Pam Nesbet, who honoured the room with cut Irish glass that lets the light through in all colours as a reminder of the seven years I had her six children in Kindergarten. Then one for Virginia Fordice, an artist who was part of the class with all her five children during the years I had them in Kindergarten. Then there was Terri Lomas, who has kept the children in dress-ups all these years. And there was one for my daughter to place in her Kindergarten, she who has helped me on every level to bring a life-giving experience to all of us in these Kindergarten days that have been mine.

After this part of the ceremony, I had asked all those who had helped me to make our garden a true jewel among gardens to sit close to the front. It was now I would unveil the first plaque to be placed on the door to the garden. Here were the names of all those who had made the garden possible: Henry Clarke; Ilse Stollar; Glenn Yoshimoto; Jenni Taylor; Carmel Lawrence; and Nancy Payne.

But the name of the Helbush family was missing: These wonderful people have for two years sent their crews in with all kinds of spectacular plants for our garden. How could I have forgotten their names? Secretly, I was blaming the engraver! Nevertheless it could be added – and it was. And now it has been put in its proper place on the door.

I wanted somehow to connect the first years of my teaching with my Kindergarten class of today. I placed six large candles to represent this 'Golden Ring'. They were placed in a circle on a small, antique stand with a circular marble top. On the other side was one of the old desks where the third-grade children I first taught would sit. As I lit each candle, I wanted to find a poem that would remind us that to reach maturity on an adult level is to again return to the six-year-old state of being – that is, at one with the wholeness of the universe. So I recited A.A. Milne's poem, 'End', which begins 'When I was one I had just begun…'

It was then time to unveil the next plaque that read: 'This room is designed and dedicated to keeping the spirit of childhood alive on every level'. I wanted this to be nailed to the door as Martin Luther had nailed his life-giving dogma to the church door. To those who follow as teachers in this room, I must admit that I had written curses that would follow anyone who brought negative, destructive philosophies, materials, dittos into this room, curses on all those who would bring plastic into this room… and on and on.

When I retired from Kindergarten teaching, I wanted to pin to the door my set of 'Ten Commandments' to keep the room holy. These 'thou shalt nots' were later changed to Blessings, and etched in brass and fixed to the door of the Kindergarten Room. But I will first reproduce those original 'shalt nots' here as they do help to convey the essence of the philosophy which I believe any holistic and empowering teacher of young children should embrace:

- Thou shalt not interfere with the natural gratitude of children.
- Thou shalt not desecrate the materials of learning and forget the role of beauty.
- Thou shall not rob children of their natural royalty.
- Thou shall not deprive children of their power to magnify the play of life.
- Thou shalt not cheat children out of the great fairy tales designed for all living.
- Thou shalt not open the classroom door on to a barren landscape.
- Thou shall not slay the imagination by intellectual and arbitrary standards.
- Thou shalt not prohibit the joy of work and accomplishment in the life of the child.
- Thou shall not forget the need to educate the parents and administration.
- Thou shalt not squelch and neglect thine own spirit.

ımandments' were designed and dedicated to keeping the
⸫ of childhood alive – and became transformed in my
ıary process into *blessings*.

⎦ so to the Blessings:

♦ Blessings on the adults of this world who realize that the young
  child needs the warmth of earthly and human experiences that feed
  the senses in order for the expansion of their adulthood.
♦ Blessings on all teachers whose gratefulness for life flows to the
  children in song and poetry.
♦ Blessings on all teachers who value the using of the finest materials
  that we call the 'tools of the gods', for the child's artistic expression.
♦ Blessings on all teachers who know the importance of crowns in the
  Kindergarten, so that the child may feel his power to rule his
  kingdom, which is himself.
♦ Blessings on all teachers who provide props and dress-ups, knowing
  that the child's true learning comes from play.
♦ Blessings on all teachers who remember that the fairy tales are the
  true religion of the child.
♦ Blessings on all teachers whose classroom is the garden, for it is here
  that all of life's lessons can be learned.
♦ Blessings on all teachers who cultivate the imagination.
♦ Blessings on all teachers who know the importance of real work in
  the life of the child.
♦ Blessings on all teachers who remember that the parents are the
  true educators of the child.
♦ Blessings on all teachers who know that to nourish their own spirit
  is the greatest gift to the child.

For my last 'thank you' of this retirement celebration, I turned to the
lullaby that we sing in Kindergarten about the Guardian Angel. I said,
'It is the Guardian Angels of your children that will now receive my
gratitude for all these years of being with us, overworked as they have
been for years. I believe in danger. I believe in disorder and I believe in
real work. When that is true, all the Guardian Angels hover. For it is at
this very point of danger that we are being met by the gods themselves,
that the formation of our very tissues, the marrow of our bones, and
the feeling of "I AM" climbs to a new life-giving level of response.

I would like you to sing it with me. Anna, my daughter, and I stand here together, for we both know how important Guardian Angels are to the Kindergarten teacher, which we are both privileged to be, she in her first year and I in my last year of Kindergarten.'

We sang it three times, for everything is done in three's in the Kindergarten. Then at the close of the last round I blew out the candles and asked everyone to join me in the garden for 'Long Life Tea'.

Memories and Experiences

Betty Peck's Kindergarten in Retrospect

It is often said that a good teacher or foundational learning experience in childhood can stay with someone for life; and in the wealth of resounding, often deeply moving 'testimonials' that follow, one could hardly ask for a more affirming commentary on the nourishment that Betty's Peck's Kindergarten children received from their experience in her loving charge.

These messages were received by Betty on the recent occasion of her eightieth birthday. Above all, what we can draw from them is a striking sense of what really matters in early childhood learning – *not* mechanistic 'early learning goals', and forced, soulless 'cognitive competencies' (the currently fashionable 'too much too soon' ideology), but rather – love, warmth, respect, and the creation of a learning and being experience that responds appropriately, imaginatively, and with intuitive wisdom to the unfolding developmental needs of each individual child. *If only* every nursery and pre-school trainee-teacher were to read, assimilate, and inwardly digest the message contained in these heart-felt commentaries on Kindergarten, it would do more to reveal to a generation of early childhood teachers the qualities necessary for nourishing early learning than any amount of didactic formalized course teaching ever could.

So, then, let us allow Betty Peck's ex-Kindergarteners to speak for themselves....

Richard House, *Series Editor*

Below are just a few of the many messages received. These and many more may be viewed online at: **www.hawthornpress.com/Betty-P/**

Adam Agee:
To be in Betty Peck's Kindergarten was to live a beautifully orchestrated dream, of which each game and chore held life meaning. The flow of life in the Kindergarten was so artistic, so pleasing to my senses. Imagine the lush green garden paths... the smell of lilac... the good taste of honey-bread we baked. We stirred the batter in a spiral like the Milky Way Galaxy we live in, and we tasted sweet maple syrup and ate apple slices cut to reveal the five-pointed star at their core. I learned that the rhythm of daily tasks is sacred, and that my deeds affect the world we live in. I suspect that my experience in Betty's Kindergarten has affected my likes and dislikes, my daily fantasies, much more than I am aware of. A great capacity for imagination and play has grown in me. For this , I am SO GRATEFUL!!!!!

Russ Agee: *(recent graduate of the Rhode Island School of Design, was in Betty's Kindergarten, 1985-6)*
I could have written a book, but I did my best to express the essence; words are woefully inadequate. Adam and I wrote separately, and yet were so pleased to discover congruity.

Life in Betty Peck's Kindergarten was exceptional in every way. Every nook and corner was filled with pleasing colors and textures; every shelf was filled with the most desirable natural play materials from Nature's abundance – sea shells, seed pods, stones; the crayons were made of colored beeswax – *oohh* did our pictures smell good! Every moment of the day was acknowledged with the joy of being alive – good morning, dear Earth, good morning dear Sun!.... The Kindergarten was alive with the hum of contented activity and all of us, parents and children alike, were invited daily to join the vibrant dance of cosmic archetypes artistically disguised as PLAY AND WORK.

A child at play in Betty Peck's Kindergarten was actually working very hard, integrating all the rich sensory input from the story-telling, singing games, outdoor garden 'maintenance', bread-making, painting, dramatic renderings of the fairy stories we heard, etc., etc., etc. – incredible! Every new day was filled with meeting its meaningful moments as they came. Yet all days reflected a well-thought-out rhythm which provided the healthy, underlying continuity for the children to be spontaneous and joyful. A perfect microcosm of the macrocosm – with all the profundity that implies – cosmic polarities, seasonal festivals, birthdays, and 'letter parties' – which gave us ample opportunity, nay, we were the joyful victims, of Betty's adamant, confident expectation to connect deeply with the roots of our most noble humanity. *Ahhh*, it's good to be Queen!

In every way, the Kindergarten spoke to the highest in all of us. In every way it nourished and cultivated our hearts, giving each what was needed and asking for one's best in return. Potent seeds for an uplifted society were planted here... and our souls were/are abloom with the true abundance of LIFE... which is LOVE.

Noor and Christa Billawala:
There are hardly enough words and hardly any wishes still missing for someone so blessed in spirit and soul; and since I am so very much indebted to you for helping me raise my young'uns (?), and since with your example you have also raised me and helped me in difficult times, and since I cannot think of a single wish unfulfilled – I wish for you the wish of your innermost longing, unknown to all but yourself; and let me be selfish and... wish for all of us that you will be with us for many many years, because we need you!

Gay and Roy Crawford:
Her influence on our life has been beyond measure.
Wisdom, kindness, love;
Nurturing to our children and our earth;
Strength, fortitude, courage of conviction –
We will always remember her values and worth.

Becky, Bill, Billy, Cal, Ty, and Sam Doty:
...Thank you for the BEST years of our life. We still remember the beautiful birthday celebrations you provided ALL of the students, Friday's bread, dressing up, and the continuity of your lesson plans. The magic of your classroom exists in our hearts today – when... both Billy and Cal (19 & 18 years old) recount the Tooth Fairy's magical entrance on that special day over 14 years ago. Thanks to your insight, Billy, who is a freshmen at Fresno State, still possesses an incredible

imagination… Ty, the baby I took everywhere with us, is a sophomore and enjoys school, participating in plays, musicals, sports, and student leadership. You are the inspiration of parents and students alike in the quest for the true education of LIFE! Thank you with all of our hearts.

David and Jessie Emanuel, David Emanuel and Maria Wamsley (and Peter & Thomas), Ken and Barbara Lawrence-Emanuel, and Kate Emanuel:
May the joy you inspired in every child who you touched reflect in your eyes and fill your heart; your presence is felt in countless families, in once and future generations.

Martin Fenster, Alexis, Sheridan and Bryce-Kurtz-Fenster, and Barbaraterry Kurtz *(in spirit):*
As the father of two of your alumni, Sheridan and Bryce Kurtz-Fenster, I have experienced first hand the lessons from the garden. Like you, they are a constant that continues to affect our lives and those around us.

Daniel Gehrs:
The world would be a different place – and a better one – if there were more people like you, Betty.

Jennifer Gehrs: *(25 years old!)*
You're still the same to me today as you were when I was in Kindergarten: timeless, beautiful, and full of life!… I had the privilege of spending two years in Betty Peck's magical presence. In those two years, I learned to find a joy and beauty in every living thing; from the clay that we crafted into cups and the fragrant yeast that made our fresh bread rise in the mornings. Those two years may have been the highlight of my entire childhood. If only every child could experience Mrs Peck!

Robin Gehrs: *(18 year devotee and former K parent 2 kids, 2 years each!)*
…thank you for all the wondrous journeys on which you have taken us… thank you for the magic you have brought into so many lives… it will be passed on for ever in an unending circle of love!

Betty and Hal Hodges:

A veritable flood tide of words comes to mind when we think of Betty Peck – among them... compassionate... creative... selfless... intuitive... innovative... gentle... calm... caring... generous... artistic... vibrant... charming....

David Lertzman, PhD:

Dear Mrs. Peck, How blessed and honoured I am to be one of the people you touched with your special way.... If you receive even one small iota of all that you have given to so many, your place is assured in Heaven... and I know that it is. I was a little boy in your Saratoga Kindergarten in 1965 and I remember you with grand affection. You loved me, and all of us SO well, and we loved you; I still do. The world shines more brightly because of you and your magic still shines in my heart, which shines now on many others. Thank you SO very much for helping me find my way in life....

God/dess Bless you All-ways and Forever, Dear, Dear Mrs Peck.

Sue, John, and Ashley Mack:

Betty Peck creates well-rounded human beings. Thanks for Ashley's good beginning!

Tom Miller:

You started me out in theatre in Kindergarten, and I learned most of what I know about acting in your backyard. What an impact one person can have on another's life. I appreciate so much what you've done for all the artistic minds in Saratoga.

Evan Parsons:

As a child, I stepped into your classroom, a place that was different, spawning an incredible creative motivation in my life. Now that I have grown, I only hope that every young child can step into such a wonderful environment and be given all that I have and all that I know. Thank you, Betty, for showing me a light most fail to see. Thank you so much! I will remember you for ever and ever. With the deepest and most intense affection.

Dean Robinson:
...one of the most lasting inspirations in my life.

Karen Robinson:
I wish... that every one of your days is filled with but a whisper of the love, inspiration, joy, and beauty that you have brought to those who have had the honor of knowing and sharing time with you.

Vicki, Richard and Melissa Schmidt:
...it's not only the children who left your Kindergarten with gold in their hearts and a sense of awe, but also we parents, too, learned so much about intrigue, wonder, and the possibilities of our daily treks.... [W]e celebrat(e) the joy you've given our family and your lessons that we remember always.

Lee, Ilse, Anina and Andreas Stollar:
...one who sees the best in everyone, has lofty visions and makes the seemingly impossible happen....

Gladys Wood Stutzman:
...a superb educator who not only instills a love for learning in her students... she constantly enriches the lives of all of us so fortunate to have known and loved her... and motivates us to try to be like her.

Alicia Teeter: *(Kindergarten baby, Neighbor, Angel, and Student)*
Not a day goes by without one of Betty Peck's teachings reappearing in my life. Every day I am reminded about how lucky I was to be the Kindergarten baby, the 'neighbor', and finally a student in Betty's Kindergarten class. To this day I make it a habit to eat strawberries and ice cream for breakfast on May Day, celebrate nature and appreciate the joys of music. Without Betty's teachings my life would not be as vivid and full as it is today – I cannot thank her enough.

Nikki Teeter:
Just how to convey the impact those magical Kindergarten years had on the lives of the Teeters, both children and adults.... Our children have grown and are now 29 and 24 years old. To this day, the experiences and lessons we shared in Betty's Kindergarten enrich our lives. My

personal favorite? Celebrate! Don't let the moments of your life and the magic of the earth pass by unnoticed.

Mary Seaver Wade:
I wish that someday soon the world will catch up to you!

David, Amy, Emily and Darby Williams:
...the greatness of the gifts you have bestowed upon us over the years:

♦ The Nursery School that has become our foundation for being the best parents we can be to our beloved children;

♦ Your love of nature and all the wonders of the world in which we live;

♦ The family traditions that have faithfully been carried on year after year: Christmas Caroling, May Day celebrations, etc.;

♦ Your devotion to children and to the child in each of us;

♦ Your ability to celebrate and see the beauty in all seasons of life;

♦ Your reminders that the world of imagination and whimsy must never be forgotten;

♦ And last but not least, your endearing presence in our lives throughout the years.

Tim Young:
Very few people are so lucky as to be given the gift of a Kindergarten experience so supportive, so loving, and so creative that it inspires in that individual a passion for life that carries them through adulthood, This experience provided by Mrs. Peck, was so much more than just a mere education. With her infinite wisdom, limitless patience and unconditional love, she turned the simplest games and activities into lessons about the most important issues in life. Lessons so filled with creativity that they inspired a young child and so profound that they continue to guide an adult today. She created an experience that was, just like her, simply magic.

Bibliography

Alliance for Childhood (2000) *Fool's Gold: A Critical Look at Computers in Childhood,* College Park, MA, USA

Armstrong, A. and Casement, C. (1955) *The Child and the Machine,* Key Porter Books, Toronto, Canada

Brennerman, R. (1983) *Fuller's Earth,* St Martin's Press, NY, USA

Campbell, D. (2000) *The Mozart Effect for Children,* William Morrow, NY, USA

Carter, R. (1988) *The Tao and Mother Goose,* The Theosophical Press, IL, USA

Chilton Pearce, J. (1992) *Evolution's End,* HarperCollins, San Francisco, CA, USA

Chilton Pearce, J. (1980) *Magical Child,* Penguin Books, NY, USA

Coplen, D. (1982) *Parenting a Path through Childhood,* Floris Books, UK

Doczi, G. (1981) *The Power of Limits,* Shambhala Publications, Boulder, CO, USA

Erikson, E. (1959) *Childhood and Society,* W W Norton & Co, NY, USA

Fentress Gardner, J. (1997) *Youth Longs to Know,* Anthroposophic Press, NY, USA

Firmage, R. (1993) *The Alphabet Abecedarium,* David R Godine, Boston, MASS, USA

Froebel, F. (2001) *Education by Development,* Froebel Foundation USA, Grand Rapids, MI, USA

Froebel, F. (2001) *Education of Man,* Froebel Foundation USA, Grand Rapids, MI, USA

Froebel, F. (2001) *Pedagogics of the Kindergarten,* Froebel Foundation USA, Grand Rapids, MI, USA

Healy, J. M. (1990) *Endangered Minds,* Simon & Schuster, NY, USA

Gardner, H. (1983) *Frames of Mind,* Basic Books Inc, NY, USA

Gilbar, S. (Ed) (1995) *Reading in Bed,* David R Godine, Boston, MASS, USA

Healy, J. M. (1998) *Failure To Connect,* Simon & Schuster, NY, USA

Heuscher, J. (1963) *The Psychiatric Study of Fairy Tales,* Charles C Thomas, Springfield, IL, USA

Hewes, D. W. (1998) *It's the Camaraderie,* University of California Center for Cooperatives, Davis, CA, USA

Jenkinson, S. (2001) *The Genius of Play*, Hawthorn Press, Stroud, UK

Kuroyanagi, T. (1982) *Totto-Chan*, Kodansha International Ltd, Tokyo

Large, M. (2003) *Set Free Childhood*, Hawthorn Press, Stroud, UK

Lovejoy, S. (1999) *Roots, Shoots, Buckets, and Boots*, Workman Publishing, NY, USA

Lovejoy, S. (1991) *Sunflower Houses*, Interweave Press, Denver, CO, USA

Lovejoy, S. (2003) *Trowel & Error*, Workman Publishing, NY, USA

May, R. (1991) *The Cry for Myth*, W W Norton & Co, NY, USA

Man, J. (2000) *Alpha Beta: How 26 Letters Shaped the Western World*, Headline, London, UK

Mellon, N. (2003) S*torytelling and the Art of Imagination*, Yellow Moon Press, MA, USA (previously Mellon, N. (1998) *The Art of Storytelling, Element*, UK)

Mellon, N. (2000) *Storytelling with Children*, Hawthorn Press, Stroud, UK

Montagu, A. (1989) *Growing Young*, Praeger Trade, USA

Montessori, M. (1967) *The Absorbent Mind*, Dell Publishing Co Inc, NY, USA

Montessori, M. (1975), *Education and Peace*, Contemporary Books Inc, USA

Murray, E. (1997) *Cultivating Sacred Space*, Pomegranate Press, San Francisco, CA, USA

O'Donohue, J. (1999) *Eternal Echoes*, HarperCollins, NY, USA

Oldfield, L. (2001) *Free to Learn*, Hawthorn Press, Stroud, UK

Pawlowski, C. (2000) *Glued to the Tube*, Sourcebooks Trade, Napperville, IL, USA

Postman, N. (1982) *The Disappearance of Childhood*, Delacorte Press, NY, USA

Rawson, M. and Rose, M. (2002) *Ready to Learn*, Hawthorn Press, Stroud, UK

Richards, M. C. (1980) *Toward Wholeness*, Wesleyan University Press, Connecticut, MASS, USA

Schneider, M. S. (1995) *A Beginner's Guide to Constructing the Universe*, Perenial Press, NY, USA

Sanders, B. (1994) *A is for Ox*, Pantheon Books, NY, USA

Shlain, L. (1999) *The Alphabet Versus the Goddess*, Penguin Group, NY, USA

Smith, F. (1978) *Understanding Reading*, Holt Rinehart Winston, NY, USA

Steiner, R. (1981) *The Renewal of Education,* Kolisko Archive, Forest Row, Sussex, UK

Stoll, C. (1999) *Heretic,* Doubleday, NY, USA

Sweet, W. and B. (1997) *Living Joyfully with Children,* Acropolis Books, Georgia, USA

Talbott, S. (1995) *The Future Does Not Compute,* Sebastopol, CA, USA

Thomson, J. (1994) *Natural Childhood,* Simon & Schuster Inc, NY, USA

Travers, P. L. (1989) *What the Bee Knows,* Penguin Books, UK

Wilson, F. R. (1999) *Hand: How Its Use Shapes the Brain, Language and Human Culture,* Knopf Publications, NY, USA

The Complete Grimm's Fairy Tales, Pantheon Books, NY, USA (1944)

A Refoundation for *the Art of Being* with Young Children

This is the story of Betty Peck's unique Kindergarten – distilling decades of experience of her work with young children. Much of the early childhood literature is dominated by formulaic contributions that are long on 'expert' didactic instruction and 'developmental force-feeding', but woefully short on inspiration. Yet many in the broad 'holistic' education movement passionately believe that *inspiration* is one of the most important qualities that teachers can bring to their relationships with children. There is certainly no substitute for the kind of rich life experience and perennial wisdom which permeate this wonderful book.

The value of *Kindergarten Education* can hardly be overestimated, offering a creative alternative to what is rapidly becoming a lost art. Far from the 'Early Learning Goals' of British early childhood education, here, by contrast, you will find heart, soul, love, tenderness, wisdom, creativity and imagination, aliveness, wholeness, reverence, and wonder. The 'art' to which I am referring, then, is *the art of being* with young children in a way that intuitively understands the subtleties of a child's learning, and the importance of adults' *sensitively attuned* enabling role in it; that respectfully nourishes their unfolding individual developmental paths; and which above all acknowledges and nurtures reverence, wonder, co-operation, and social and emotional intelligence.

Here, then, we find a refreshing alternative to the instrumental, utilitarian learning which has recently swamped early childhood education in the developed world. This book beautifully describes just what it is possible to create in the Kindergarten, and we should be deeply grateful to Betty Peck for championing what is rapidly becoming a dying art by creating a book which communicates the very 'soul' of Kindergarten teaching in the midst of this bleak, utilitarian age.

At its best, the Kindergarten is far more *an extension of the home, family life* than it is a formal setting for formalised learning. With the notable exception of the Steiner (Waldorf) movement, this 'home extension' is being increasingly lost in Britain, with its centrally imposed 'quasi-curriculum'. For these tender years Betty Peck clearly believes in the central place of *community*, with an associated enveloping love and warmth. Rudolf Steiner's 'Motto of the Social Ethic' is most apposite here: 'The healthy social life is found when in the mirror of each human soul the whole community finds its reflection, and when in the community the virtue of each one is living' – a motto which could be an inspiring maxim for the kind of living, loving, family-centred Kindergarten described in this book.

Above all, Betty Peck's *love of celebration* overflows throughout – her deep understanding of the way in which it nourishes the young child, and helps to confer a meaning upon, and reverence for, life which will stay with the child for the whole of her life. This book provides the reader with a wonderful 'initiation' into the importance and the practicalities of celebrating life in all its facets, without which children's – and our – existence would be immeasurably impoverished.

The Western world currently seems to be passing through an extraordinarily anti-spiritual, materialistic phase. In the face of the deadening impact of these soulless values, many practitioners are *crying out for* the inspiration and wisdom that a crude 'modernity' is doing its best to extinguish, and which only a lively communion with the natural world and the deepest of human experience can provide.

Distinguished American Kindergarten teacher Betty Peck's new book *Kindergarten Education* is for anyone who wants to infuse their early-years practice with love, beauty, truth, wisdom, and inspiration. It is positively brim-full with ideas, anecdotes, creativity, imagination, and 'soul'. As Betty herself so aptly writes, 'The teacher is responsible for keeping alive the magic [of learning], in whatever form she can manage'. Certainly, for any early childhood educator looking for the kind of soul nourishment that should surely be the life-blood of all nursery and Kindergarten teachers, I cannot commend this book too highly.

Richard House
Hawthorn Press
Early Years Series Editor

Other Books from Hawthorn Press

Free to Learn
Introducing Steiner Waldorf early
childhood education
LYNNE OLDFIELD

Free to Learn is a comprehensive introduction to
Steiner Waldorf kindergartens for parents,
educators and early years' students. Lynne
Oldfield illustrates the theory and practice of
kindergarten education with stories, helpful
insights and lively observations.

*'Children are allowed freedom to be active within acceptable boundaries;
who are in touch with their senses and the environment; who are self
assured but not over confident; who are developing their readiness to receive
a formal education – in short, children who are free to be children and
"free to learn".'*

Kate Adams, *International Journal of Children's Spirituality*
256pp; 216 x 138mm; 1 903458 06 4; pb

The Genius of Play
Celebrating the spirit of childhood
SALLY JENKINSON

The Genius of Play addresses what play is, why it matters, and how
modern life endangers children's play. Sally Jenkinson's amusing, vivid
observations will delight parents and teachers wanting to explore the
never-ending secrets of children's play.

*'Enchanting photos and vignettes of young children at play ... do enjoy the
account of the 'wedding dress den' and the old Suffolk recipes for 'preserving
children.'*
Marian Whitehead, *Nursery World*
224pp; 216 x 138mm; 1 903458 04 8; pb

Muddles, Puddles and Sunshine

Your activity book to help when someone has died

WINSTON'S WISH

'Sensitively done and redolent with true insight into children.'
Caduceus

Muddles, Puddles and Sunshine offers practical and sensitive support for bereaved children. Beautifully illustrated, it gives a helpful series of activities and exercises accompanied by the friendly characters of Bee and Bear.

32pp; 297 x 210mm landscape; illustrations; 1 869 890 58 2; pb

Helping Children to Overcome Fear

The healing power of play

RUSSELL EVANS

'This inspirational book should become mandatory reading for Paediatricians and Play Therapists... indeed any adult who is serious in their desire to be alongside a child needing to face their fear. It gently embraces the skills of respectful listening, creativity and fun – instantly recognisable to a discerning child.'

Julie Stokes, Consultant Psychologist, Founder of Winston's Wish, a Grief Support Programme for Children

128pp; 216 x 138mm; 1 903458 02 1; pb

Ready to Learn

From birth to school readiness

MARTYN RAWSON AND MICHAEL ROSE

Ready to Learn will help you to decide when your child is ready to take the step from kindergarten to school proper. The key is an imaginative grasp of how children aged 0-6 years learn to play, speak, think and relate between birth and six years of age.

'Sound points about the risks of making developmentally inappropriate demands, including the headlong rush to get children to read and write ever earlier.' Jennie Lindon, *Nursery World*

192pp; 216 x 138mm; 1 903458 15 3; pb

Set Free Childhood

Parents' survival guide to coping with computers and TV

MARTIN LARGE

Children watch TV and use computers for five hours daily on average. The result? Record levels of learning difficulties, obesity, eating disorders, sleep problems, language delay, aggressive behaviour, anxiety – and children on fast forward. However, *Set Free Childhood* shows you how to counter screen culture and create a calmer, more enjoyable family life.

'A comprehensive, practical and readable guide… the skilful interplay between academic research and anecdotal evidence engages the reader.'

Jane Morris-Brown, *Steiner Education*

240pp; 216 x 138mm; 1 903458 43 9; pb

*y*telling with Children

NANCY MELLON

Telling stories awakens wonder and creates special occasions with children, whether it is bedtime, around the fire or on rainy days. Nancy Mellon shows how you can become a confident storyteller.

'Nancy Mellon continues to be an inspiration for storytellers old and new. Her experience, advice and suggestions work wonders. They are potent seeds that give you the creative confidence to find your own style of storytelling.'

Ashley Ramsden, Director of the School
of Storytelling, Emerson College

192pp; 216 x 138mm; illustrations; 1 903458 08 0 ; pb

The Singing Day

Songbook and CD for singing with young children

CANDY VERNEY

Singing with babies is one of the joys of being a parent. It is a lifetime gift from you that children love. This easy to use songbook and CD offer practical help for singing with young children from birth to 4 years old.

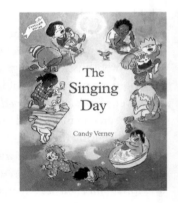

'Opens our eyes to all the opportunities for singing that arise in a child's day, giving encouragement as well as practical tips.'

Caroline White,
Stream of Sound Choir

160pp; 250 x 200mm; 1 903458 25 0; pb/CD

Celebrating Christmas Together

Nativity and Three Kings Plays with Stories and Songs

ESTELLE BRYER AND JANNI NICOL

This Christmas treasury includes – the Nativity Play; how to create a Crib scene; making an Advent Calendar; the Three Kings Play and some Christmas stories.

'A practical and beautiful guide to making Christmas a magical time for children.'
    Sally Jenkinson, author of *The Genius of Play*

96pp; 210 x 148mm; 1 903458 20 X; pb;

Christmas Stories Together

ESTELLE BRYER AND JANNI NICOL

This is a treasure trove of 36 tales for children aged 3-9, with stories ranging from Advent and Christmas to the Holy Family's flight into Egypt. These stories soon become family favourites, with their imaginative yet down to earth language.

'Alight with the genius of storytelling. It tenderly shows how to weave a pattern of stories over Advent and the twelve days of Christmas.'
                Nancy Mellon, author of
                Storytelling with Children

128pp; 210 x 148mm; 1 903458 22 6; pb

the Other One!

String Games and Stories Book 1

MICHAEL TAYLOR

This well-traveled and entertaining series of tales is accompanied by clear instructions and explanatory diagrams – guaranteed not to tie you in knots and will teach you tricks with which to dazzle your friends! With something for everyone, these ingenious tricks and tales are developed and taught with utter simplicity, making them suitable from age 5 upwards.

'When we go wrong playing Cat's Cradle, we call it Dog's Cradle!'

Megan Gain, aged 6, London

128pp; 216 x 148mm; drawings; 1 869 890 49 3; pb

Now you see it...

String Games and Stories Book 2

MICHAEL TAYLOR

String games are fun, inviting children to exercise skill, imagination and teamwork. They give hands and fingers something clever and artistic to do! Following the success of *Pull the Other One!,* here are more of Michael Taylor's favourite string games, ideal for family travel, for creative play and for party tricks.

136pp; 216 x 148mm; 1 903458 21 8; pb

Games Children Play

How games and sport help children develop

KIM JOHN PAYNE

This comprehensive games handbook is for playing with children and teenagers. These games are tried and tested favourites. Children's growth is explored through movement, fun, play, songs and games. Each game is clearly described, with helpful illustrations, guidance on the age appropriateness of games and an explanation of how games help child growth.

192pp; 297 x 210mm; 1 869 890 78 7; pb

Kinder Dolls

A Waldorf doll-making handbook

MARICRISTIN SEALEY

Children treasure handmade dolls. *Kinder Dolls* shows how to create handcrafted dolls from natural materials. A range of simple, colourful designs will inspire both beginners and experienced doll makers alike. These dolls are old favourites, originating in Waldorf Steiner kindergartens where parents make dolls together for their children, and for the school.

'*A fine source for the beginner doll maker. It is a valuable primer, full of practical tips, simple designs and clear, easy to follow instructions.*'

Sara McDonald, *Magic Cabin Dolls*

160pp; 246 x 189mm; 1 903458 03 X; pb

The Children's Year

Seasonal crafts and clothes

STEPHANIE COOPER, CHRISTINE FYNES-CLINTON, MARIJE ROWLING

This well illustrated book with clear instructions shows parents and children how to make projects step by step. Designs for children's clothing are included, using natural fabrics. Here are soft toys, wooden toys, moving toys such as balancing birds or climbing gnomes, horses, woolly hats, mobiles and dolls. There are over 100 projects to make relating to the seasons of the year.

'Another brilliant book from Hawthorn. Suitable for all ages and level of crafts skill.'

The Mother Magazine

192pp; 250 x 200mm; 1 869 890 00 0; pb

Festivals Together

Guide to multicultural celebration

SUE FITZJOHN, MINDA WESTON, JUDY LARGE

You can celebrate festivals from cultures from all over the world with *Festivals Together!* This resource guide offers 26 Buddhist, Christian, Hindu, Jewish, Muslim and Sikh festivals. There are stories, things to make, recipes, songs, customs and activities for each festival. You will be able to share in the adventures of Anancy the spider trickster, how Ganesh got his elephant head and share in Eid, Holi, Wesak, Advent, Divali, Chinese New Year and more.

'The ideal book for anyone who wants to tackle multicultural festivals.'

Nursery World

224pp; 250 x 200mm; 1 869 890 46 9; pb;

Festivals, Family and Food

Guide to seasonal celebration

DIANA CAREY AND JUDY LARGE

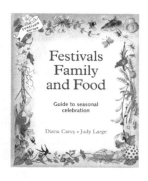

This family favourite is a unique, well loved source of stories, recipes, things to make, activities, poems, songs and festivals. Each festival such as Christmas, Candlemas and Martinmas has its own, well-illustrated chapter. There are also sections on Birthdays, Rainy Days, Convalescence and a Birthday Calendar. The perfect present for a family or a teacher's resource, it explores the numerous festivals that children love celebrating.

'*Every family should have one.*'   *Daily Mail*

224pp; 250 x 200mm; illustrations; 0 950 706 23 X; pb

All Year Round

Christian calendar of celebrations

ANN DRUITT, CHRISTINE FYNES-CLINTON,

MARIJE ROWLING

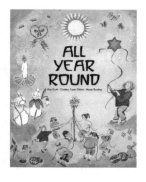

All Year Round offers crafts to make, activities, seasonal stories, poems and songs to share with your family. It is full of well-illustrated ideas for celebration, from Candlemas to Christmas and Midsummer to the Winter solstice. Each festival has a special character of its own that brings a gift to the whole family.

320pp; 250 x 200mm; 1 869 890 47 7; pb

The Islamic Year

Surahs, Stories and Celebrations

NOORAH AL-GAILANI AND CHRIS SMITH

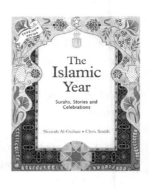

Celebrate Muslim festivals with this inspiring treasury of stories, surahs, songs, games, recipes, craft and art activities! Folk tales illustrate the core values of Islamic culture with gentle humour and wisdom. *The Islamic Year* is beautifully illustrated by Helen Williams, with a colouring calendar, Arabic calligraphy of the Names of God, traditional patterns, maps and pictures.

'The festivals are explained in a simple and clear way, relating them to each aspect of the Prophet's life and teaching.'

Baroness Uddin, House of Lords, Westminster

240pp; 250 x 200mm; 1 903458 14 5; pb

Celebrating Irish Festivals

Calendar of seasonal celebrations

RUTH MARSHALL

If you are interested in Irish traditions, need a family or school resource, then here is an inspiring treasury of stories, beautiful illustrations, poems, traditions, food, activities, games, dances and songs. Reaching back to the ancient festivals of Imbolc, Bealtaine, Lughnasadh, Samhain, and to Celtic Christianity – Ruth Marshall also offers new ways for engaging children.

'A comprehensive calendar of festivals that children will cherish.'

Irelands Own, Summer 2003

224pp; 250 x 200mm; 1 903458 23 4; pb

Getting in touch with Hawthorn Press

We would be delighted to receive your feedback on Kindergarten Education.

Visit our website for details of the Education and Early Years Series and books for parents, plus forthcoming books and events:

http://www.hawthornpress.com

Ordering books

If you have difficulties ordering Hawthorn Press books from a bookshop, you can order online at **www.hawthornpress.com** or you can order direct from:

United Kingdom
Booksource
32 Finlas Street, Glasgow
G22 5DU
Tel: (08702) 402182
Fax: (0141) 557 0189
E-mail: orders@booksource.net

USA/North America
Steiner Books
PO Box 960, Herndon
VA 20172-0960
Tel: (800) 856 8664
Fax: (703) 661 1501
E-mail: service@steinerbooks.org

Dear Reader

If you wish to follow up your reading of this book, please tick the boxes below as appropriate, fill in your name and address and return to Hawthorn Press:

☐ Please send me a catalogue of other Hawthorn Press books.

☐ Please send me details of Early Years events and courses.

Questions I have about the Early Years are:

_____

_____

_____

_____

_____

Name _____

Address _____

_____

_____

Postcode _____ Tel. no. _____

Please return to: Hawthorn Press, Hawthorn House,
1 Lansdown Lane, Stroud, Glos. GL5 1BJ, UK
or Fax (01453) 751138

kgt